JUDGES
FROM START2FINISH

MICHAEL WHITWORTH

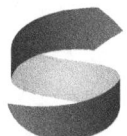

© 2025 by Start2Finish

All rights reserved. No part of this publication may be reproduced, stored in a retrieval system, or transmitted in any form or by any means without the prior written permission of the author. The only exception is brief quotations in printed reviews.

ISBN 978-1-941972-91-5

Published by Start2Finish
Bend, Oregon 97702
start2finish.org

Printed in the United States of America

Unless otherwise noted, all Scripture quotations are from The Holy Bible, English Standard Version®, copyright © 2001 by Crossway Bibles, a publishing ministry of Good News Publishers. Used by permission. All rights reserved.

Cover Design: Evangela Creative

CONTENTS

1. The Roots & Cycle of Rebellion — 5
2. God's Unexpected Deliverers — 11
3. Strength Through Faith — 17
4. The Crisis of Faith — 23
5. Gideon's Triumph & Tragedy — 29
6. The Peril of Self-Exaltation — 35
7. The Folly of Rash Faith — 41
8. Called but Compromised — 48
9. Set Apart but Set Adrift — 55
10. The Corruption of Private Religion — 62
11. The Chaos of Self-Rule — 69
12. No King but God — 76

1

THE ROOTS & CYCLE OF REBELLION

JUDGES 1:1-3:6

Objective: To see how Israel's partial obedience led to rebellion and learn the danger of compromise.

INTRODUCTION

The opening chapters of Judges tell one of Scripture's most sobering stories—the slow decay of faith that followed Israel's brightest hour. After Joshua's death, the nation stood on the edge of promise and peril. God had given them the land and the command to possess it fully, yet they hesitated, compromised, and settled for less than obedience. What began as small concessions—alliances, coexistence, and incomplete victories—soon grew into moral erosion and national apostasy. The people who once followed God's voice now followed the gods of their neighbors.

This lesson explores how partial obedience became the root of Israel's spiritual decline and established the destructive rhythm that defines the book of Judges: rebellion, retribution, repentance, and restoration. The same pattern warns believers today that divided loyalty cannot coexist with genuine devotion. God does not bless selective faithfulness; He calls his people to complete surrender.

Through Israel's early failures, we learn that disobedience rarely begins with open defiance—it begins with rationalized compromise. When faith is not fully practiced and passed on, it withers into forgetfulness and sin.

EXAMINATION

The introduction to Judges traces Israel's decline from initial faithfulness to entrenched compromise. It began with a hopeful spirit but ends with deep moral decay. This section functions as both prologue and warning—showing how the failure to obey fully led to spiritual ruin.

1. A promising beginning (1:1-2)

The people began well by seeking God's direction after Joshua's death. The question itself showed humility and dependence: "Who shall go up first for us?" God answered clearly, appointing Judah to lead. The promise, "I have given the land into his hand" reminded them that victory rested on divine strength, not human numbers. Judah's tribe, symbolizing leadership and courage, was to act first. Israel seemed ready to follow the Lord's word.

2. Early successes and small compromises (1:3-20)

Judah invited Simeon to join their campaign—a reasonable alliance but a subtle shift from complete trust in God's sufficiency. They won battles and captured cities, but cracks formed in their faith. The story of Adoni-bezek shows that God's justice works through human hands; yet the gruesome details underscores that Israel was beginning to adopt the cruelty of its enemies. Even in victory, moral boundaries blurred.

Caleb's conquest of Hebron and Othniel's bravery reminded readers of earlier faithfulness, but the refrain "they could not drive out" begins to echo. The mention of iron chariots in verse 19 revealed fear and rationalization: God had promised victory, but Israel measured success by visible odds. Partial obedience became the seed of future rebellion.

3. The geography of disobedience (1:21-36)

From this point, the narrator moves tribe by tribe, documenting failure after failure. Benjamin did not expel the Jebusites; Manasseh, Ephraim, Zebulun, Asher, and Naphtali all compromised. The language shifts from "did not drive out" to "lived among." Coexistence replaced conquest. What began as obedience became convenience. The tribes chose labor and profit over holiness, pressing Canaanites into servitude instead of removing them. They saw opportunity where God saw danger.

This catalogue of disobedience was more than history—it was theology in geography. Each tribe's failure marked another boundary of faith lost. God had drawn the lines of their inheritance, but they redrew them by compromise. The land that was to reflect God's holiness became infected by pagan influence. The cancer of compromise spread northward until no tribe was untouched.

4. The angel's rebuke (2:1-5)

When divine messengers appear in Scripture, their words demand attention. This one spoke as though God himself stood among them: "I brought you up from Egypt ... I said, 'I will never break my covenant with you.' ... But you have not obeyed my voice." The rebuke struck at the heart of the issue—God's covenant was unbreakable, but Israel's obedience was optional in their minds. Because they chose coexistence over consecration, the Lord declared that the remaining nations would become "thorns in your sides" and their gods a snare.

The people responded with tears, naming the place Bokim, "weeping." Yet there is no record of reform. Emotion replaced repentance. They offered sacrifices, but the heart of their devotion remained unchanged. Tears without transformation are powerless to stop decline.

5. A generation that forgot (2:6-10)

The next paragraph contrasts sharply with Joshua's faithful generation. Those who saw God's mighty works died, and their children grew up without firsthand knowledge of his deliverance. The failure here was not merely moral—it was parental and spiritual. Israel's leaders fought battles but neglected to teach hearts. They enjoyed the blessings but failed to transmit the story of grace. Faith that is not taught and modeled will not survive transition.

This pattern repeats throughout Scripture. One generation knows God's power; the next only hears of it; the third forget it entirely. Judges 2:10 stands as one of the saddest verses in the Bible: "There arose another generation after them who did not know the LORD." Forgetfulness is the soil of idolatry.

6. The cycle of sin began (2:11-3:6)

What follows becomes the template for the entire book—a tragic rhythm of rebellion, retribution, repentance, and restoration. Israel turned to Baal and Ashtaroth, worshiping fertility gods of Canaan. This was not casual curiosity; it was spiritual adultery. God's anger burned, and he allowed oppressors to overrun them. Yet even in his wrath, grace was present: "The LORD raised up judges, who saved them."

The term "judge" here does not mean courtroom arbitrator but deliverer—a leader through whom God rescued his people. However, the relief was temporary. As soon as the judge died, the people returned to corruption, often worse than before. Sin deepened; repentance shortened. What began as occasional rebellion became habitual idolatry.

Judges 3:1-6 explains that God left certain nations to test Israel's fidelity. These pagan groups became living tests—would Israel obey or assimilate? Tragically, they intermarried and adopted foreign worship. The separation between God's people and the world collapsed completely. The section ends as it began—with compromise breeding captivity.

The introduction thus reveals a sobering truth: decline rarely begins with defiance; it begins with half-hearted faith. The nation's first failure was not losing battles but losing conviction. When God's people stopped driving sin out of their lives, that sin eventually drove them away from God.

APPLICATION

1. Partial obedience is total disobedience

Israel's downfall began not with rebellion but with rationalization. They told themselves partial obedience was enough. Modern believers often make the same mistake—negotiating obedience, excusing sin, or calling compromise "balance." God desires complete surrender, not selective devotion (see Matt. 6:24; 7:21-23). Small concessions to sin eventually enslave the heart. The Christian life cannot coexist with what God commands us to crucify. If we manage sin instead of mortifying it, it will master us. Every area of incomplete obedience today becomes tomorrow's source of spiritual defeat.

2. Faith must be re-taught to every generation

Judges warns us that faith is never inherited; it must be personally embraced (see 2 Tim. 1:5). The tragedy of Israel's children forgetting the Lord reveals the necessity of intentional discipleship. Parents and church leaders must tell God's stories often and live them authentically. Doctrine must be modeled as much as taught. A generation that enjoys the fruit of past faithfulness but fails to plant new seeds will soon face famine. Every believer has a sacred duty to hand down not only biblical information but living conviction. When we neglect to pass on the faith, we unintentionally prepare the next generation for idolatry.

3. God's discipline is a sign of his mercy

God's decision to leave pagan nations among Israel was not abandonment but mercy. He desired their repentance more than their ruin. In the same way, God sometimes allows hardship, temptation, or lingering struggle to test and refine us. His discipline exposes divided hearts and calls us back to obedience. Pain becomes the instrument of grace when it drives us to dependence. The believer who resists God's correction misunderstands his love (Heb. 12:5-11). The thorns and snares of life are reminders that holiness matters. Discipline, though unpleasant, proves that God still cares enough to confront our compromise.

CONCLUSION

Israel's story in these opening chapters reminds us that decline begins not with defiance but with compromise. Partial obedience blurred the lines of faith until disobedience became a way of life. God's people wept over their sin but did not turn from it, proving that emotion without repentance changes nothing. Yet even in failure, the Lord remained faithful—testing, teaching, and preparing to deliver them once again.

As the narrative turns to Judges 3:7-31, God's mercy takes center stage. He raises up deliverers—ordinary people empowered by his Spirit—to rescue a disobedient nation. Through Othniel, Ehud, and Shamgar, we will see how God's grace works through both faithfulness and frailty to accomplish his purpose and preserve his covenant.

REFLECTION

1. How did Israel's early victories reveal subtle compromises?
2. What does the geography of failure teach about gradual disobedience?
3. Why was the angel's rebuke both just and merciful?
4. How did one generation's forgetfulness lead to national idolatry?
5. What purpose did the remaining nations serve in testing Israel?

DISCUSSION

1. What modern examples show partial obedience today?
2. How can families better transmit faith to the next generation?
3. In what ways has God's discipline restored your obedience?
4. Why is compromise often more dangerous than open rebellion?
5. How can believers break recurring cycles of sin?

2

GOD'S UNEXPECTED DELIVERERS

JUDGES 3:7-31

Objective: To see how God delivers his people through ordinary, Spirit-empowered servants in extraordinary ways.

INTRODUCTION

The book of Judges continues to unfold God's faithfulness against the backdrop of Israel's failure. After the nation's partial obedience led to spiritual decline, God's people once again found themselves trapped in cycles of sin and oppression. Yet even in their rebellion, the Lord did not abandon them. Instead, he raised up unexpected deliverers—ordinary men through whom his extraordinary power was displayed.

Judges 3:7-31 introduces the first three of these unlikely heroes: Othniel, Ehud, and Shamgar. Each represented a different kind of servant, yet all proved that God's strength was not limited by human weakness. Othniel stood as the model of Spirit-filled faithfulness; Ehud, the left-handed liberator, accomplished deliverance through cunning and courage; and Shamgar, armed with nothing but a farmer's tool, struck down the enemies of God's people. Through them, the Lord reminded Israel—and us—that deliverance belongs to him alone.

This lesson challenges us to see how God often chooses the unexpected to accomplish his will. His purposes are not hindered by background, skill, or circumstance. What he requires is availability and faith.

EXAMINATION

Judges 3:7-31 presented the first three deliverers God raised to rescue his people. Each account revealed something unique about God's character and Israel's condition. The stories progressed from model obedience to moral complexity, showing both the faithfulness of God and the growing corruption of Israel.

1. Othniel: The model deliverer (3:7-11)

The narrative opened with a familiar diagnosis: "Israel did what was evil in the sight of the LORD." Idolatry again replaced faith, and God allowed Cushan-Rishathaim, king of Aram-naharaim, to oppress them for eight years. Yet when Israel cried out, the Lord raised Othniel, Caleb's younger brother. His family connection recalled Israel's faithful past, linking him to one who wholly followed the Lord.

Othniel's story was concise because it was uncomplicated. "The Spirit of the Lord came upon him," and he went to war. There were no tricks, negotiations, or doubts. His strength came not from strategy but from the Spirit. The result was total victory and forty years of peace.

Othniel embodied the pattern of ideal deliverance—faithful servant, Spirit-empowered mission, divine success. The Spirit's role was central. God's people could accomplish nothing apart from his power. This story set the standard for all that followed. Later judges departed from this simplicity; their character flaws mirrored Israel's spiritual decline. Yet in Othniel we glimpse God's design for his people: humble dependence, divine empowerment, lasting peace.

2. Ehud: The clever liberator (3:12-30)

With Othniel's death, the nation again turned to evil. God delivered them into the hand of Eglon, king of Moab. This time the oppression lasted eighteen years. But again, when the people cried out, "the LORD raised up for them a deliverer, Ehud, the son of Gera, the Benjaminite, a left-handed man." The description is more than physical detail; it foreshadowed the irony of the story. The right hand was a symbol of power and skill. Ehud's left-handedness, whether literal or symbolic of weakness, highlighted God's ability to use what the world considered inferior.

Ehud fashioned a double-edged sword and hid it on his right thigh, the unexpected side. He brought tribute to Eglon, a corpulent and complacent king. After delivering the payment, Ehud returned to the king under the pretext of a secret message. When Eglon dismissed his attendants, Ehud struck swiftly, plunging the sword deep into the king's belly. The narrator's vivid details—Eglon's girth, the closed doors, the oblivious servants—added both realism and dark humor. The author wanted readers to see divine irony: the mighty oppressor was slain by an unexpected hand in an unexpected way.

Ehud escaped, rallied Israel at the Jordan, and led them to victory over Moab. Ten thousand enemies fell, and "the land had rest for eighty years." While his methods were unorthodox, his courage was undeniable. God's Spirit worked through creative, even surprising, means. Ehud's story reminds us that deliverance often comes through those willing to act decisively when others remain afraid.

Yet this account also reveals the growing moral ambiguity in Israel's leadership. Othniel's victory was straightforward and Spirit-led; Ehud's involved deception and violence. The judge's cunning reflected Israel's own complexity—a nation still dependent on God but increasingly influenced by the world's values. Still, God's grace worked through flawed instruments to accomplish perfect purposes.

3. Shamgar: The brief but bold deliverer (3:31)

The final verse of the chapter shift abruptly: "After him was Shamgar the son of Anath, who killed 600 of the Philistines with an oxgoad, and he also saved Israel." Nothing else is said. Yet the brevity of the account underscores the theme of divine sovereignty. Shamgar's name and title suggest a non-Israelite origin—perhaps a Canaanite or foreign mercenary. If so, God's use of him was even more remarkable.

The oxgoad, a simple farmer's tool, was not a weapon of war. Its mention highlights both Shamgar's courage and God's enabling power. Six hundred Philistines fell not by sword but by a stick in the hands of a willing man. Like David's sling or Moses' staff, the oxgoad became a symbol of what God could do through unlikely means.

Shamgar's story also foreshadowed the growing threat of the Philistines, who would later dominate Israel's history through Samson, Samuel, and David. His act of deliverance, though small, was vital—it preserved Israel's survival during a dangerous era.

4. The theological thread

Across these three judges runs a consistent theological pattern: God raised, empowered, and delivered. Human weakness never hindered divine strength. Whether through the faithful Othniel, the cunning Ehud, or the obscure Shamgar, salvation belongs to the Lord. The diversity of these deliverers teaches that God's Spirit works through many personalities and methods, yet the goal is always the same—his glory and his people's freedom.

At the same time, the progression from Othniel's simplicity to Ehud's complexity marked the beginning of Israel's spiritual descent. God remained constant, but his instruments grew increasingly flawed. The lesson is clear: God's mercy continues even as his people unravel. He works not because they deserve it, but because his covenant love endures.

APPLICATION

1. God uses ordinary people for extraordinary work

Othniel, Ehud, and Shamgar show that divine calling is not limited by human ability. God delights in using what seems weak or unqualified to demonstrate his strength. Whether you feel ordinary, overlooked, or ill-equipped, you are not unusable (1 Cor. 1:26-29). The Spirit who empowered these judges still empowers believers today to resist evil and serve courageously (Eph 3:20). God's question is not, "Are you strong?" but, "Are you available?" Ordinary obedience in the hands of an extraordinary God changes history.

2. Spiritual victory requires divine empowerment

The difference between Othniel's victory and Israel's earlier defeat was the Spirit's presence. Every triumph in the Christian life begins with dependence on the Holy Spirit. Human courage and cleverness accomplish nothing lasting apart from divine power. We must daily yield to the Spirit's guidance and strength, trusting him for both wisdom and endurance. Spiritual battles cannot be fought with physical weapons or human logic. Only when God's Spirit fills our hearts can we overcome sin's oppression and experience peace (Rom. 8:11). Victory flows not from our might but from his indwelling power.

3. God's deliverance is creative and surprising

Ehud's left hand and Shamgar's oxgoad remind us that God's deliverance rarely comes as expected. His methods overturn human logic so that his glory remains unmistakable. Sometimes he uses unlikely people, unconventional means, or unexpected timing to accomplish his plan. When we face obstacles that seem overwhelming, we must remember that the Lord specializes in impossible situations. Faith waits for his wisdom instead of dictating his methods. The God who saved Israel through unexpected instruments still works creatively in our lives today, proving that nothing is too small or strange for his redemptive hand.

CONCLUSION

Through Othniel, Ehud, and Shamgar, Israel learned that God's deliverance did not depend on strength, status, or strategy but on his Spirit working through willing hearts. Each judge demonstrated a different way God uses ordinary people to accomplish extraordinary purposes. Othniel showed faithful simplicity, Ehud embodied courageous ingenuity, and Shamgar revealed fearless determination. Together, they proved that divine power often works through human weakness (2 Cor. 12:9).

As the story of Judges continues, Israel's need for courageous leadership only grows deeper. Lesson 3 will show how God again chose unexpected servants—this time a woman, Deborah, and a hesitant warrior, Barak—to defeat mighty oppressors. Their story will remind us that faith, not force, determines victory, and that God's strength shines brightest through those who trust and obey.

REFLECTION

1. How does Othniel model Spirit-empowered leadership?
2. What does Ehud's story reveal about God's creativity?
3. Why might God choose a non-Israelite like Shamgar?
4. How does this passage mark Israel's moral decline?
5. What common thread links all three deliverers?

DISCUSSION

1. How can you be "available" for God's work?
2. Why is spiritual power more vital than strategy?
3. How has God surprised you through unexpected answers?
4. What "ordinary tools" might God use in your service?
5. How can faith replace fear in daily obedience?

3

STRENGTH THROUGH FAITH

JUDGES 4-5

Objective: To encourage courageous obedience that trusts God's power in the face of fear and opposition.

INTRODUCTION

The story of Deborah, Barak, and Jael stands as one of the most remarkable displays of faith and courage in Judges. After repeated cycles of sin and oppression, Israel once again cried out for deliverance. Yet this time, God's answer came through surprising instruments—a prophetess, a hesitant warrior, and a courageous woman armed with a tent peg. Their story reminds us that God's power is not bound by gender, strength, or circumstance. He honors those who trust his word and act with courageous obedience.

In a time when fear ruled and faith faltered, Deborah's confidence in God ignited a movement of deliverance. Her bold leadership inspired Barak to step forward in faith, and their obedience together brought victory over Sisera's mighty army. Jael's unexpected act completed God's plan and fulfilled prophecy, demonstrating how divine power works through human faithfulness.

This lesson calls believers to the same kind of courage—to act on God's promises even when the odds seem overwhelming. True faith does not wait for perfect conditions; it moves forward in trust that God will accomplish his purpose.

EXAMINATION

1. Israel's need and God's call (4:1-7)

Israel's sin again brought oppression. Jabin ruled from Hazor, the same city Joshua once burned (Josh. 11:13), showing that Israel's past victories had faded through complacency. God allowed Sisera to dominate them until their cries reached heaven. Even in discipline, the Lord's compassion remained. His mercy always outran his people's failures.

Deborah emerged as a prophetess and judge—roles that combined spiritual discernment with administrative leadership. She sat beneath "the palm of Deborah" in Ephraim, where people came for counsel and justice. In an era when few listened to God, He spoke through her. When God chose to deliver Israel, He did not seek a new Joshua or a skilled warrior but a faithful listener. God's calling of Deborah reminds us that leadership is first a matter of obedience, not gender, status, or strength.

Deborah sent for Barak of Naphtali and delivered the Lord's command: "Go, gather [10,000 men], and I will [Sisera] him into your hand." God's promise was explicit, but Barak hesitated. Fear eclipsed faith. He wanted visible assurance—Deborah's presence—as if her faith might compensate for his weakness. Yet Deborah agreed to go, not out of indulgence, but partnership. Her courage inspired his obedience. Still, she warned him that the honor would go to a woman, for faithless hesitation forfeits full glory.

2. The battle belonged to the Lord (4:8-16)

When Deborah and Barak marched to Mount Tabor, Sisera gathered his army at the Kishon River. The valley favored chariots, not foot soldiers. From every human perspective, Israel's forces faced certain defeat. Yet Deborah declared, "Up! For this is the day in which the LORD has given Sisera into your hand." Her words revealed the essence of faith—seeing God's promise as already fulfilled. She led with prophetic confidence while Barak advanced in trust.

At that moment, God intervened. Judges 5:20-21 interprets the event poetically: "From heaven the stars fought, . … The torrent Kishon swept them away." Likely a sudden storm turned the battleground into a swamp, neutralizing the chariots. What Israel could not do by might, God accomplished through creation. The Lord of heaven fought for his people, proving again that victory did not depend on numbers or technology, but on obedience and faith.

Barak pursued the enemy relentlessly until no man remained. His courage, once timid, grew bold through obedience. Faith does not always start strong, but it strengthens with every step of trust. The victory belonged to God, yet he allowed his servants to share in the triumph. When they obeyed despite fear, they experienced his power in ways impossible to those who held back.

3. Jael's courage and the fulfillment of prophecy (4:17-22)

While the armies clashed, Sisera fled on foot to the tent of Jael, wife of Heber the Kenite. Her family lived in peace with Jabin, so Sisera assumed safety. Jael welcomed him, offered milk, and covered him with a blanket. When he slept, she drove a tent peg through his temple, killing him instantly. The act was shocking, but it fulfilled Deborah's prophecy: the honor would go to a woman.

Jael's deed was not random violence but a decisive act of allegiance to God's cause. In a time when men hesitated, women led with faith and courage. Deborah listened to God's voice; Jael acted upon it. The Lord used both to humble Israel's enemies and remind his people that deliverance came from unexpected sources.

4. Worship after the war (5:1-31)

The victory inspired one of the most beautiful hymns in Scripture—the "Song of Deborah." It celebrates God's intervention and honored those who "offered themselves willingly." The song reveals that leadership and courage are spiritual sacrifices. Tribes like Zebulun and Naphtali were praised for risking their lives, while others were rebuked for staying home. God's people are always divided between those who act in faith and those who remain comfortable in safety.

The song portrays God as a divine warrior. "The earth trembled and the heavens dropped. ... The mountains quaked before the LORD." Creation itself responded to his command. Deborah's worship transformed history into theology—she interpreted victory as God's self-revelation. Jael was celebrated as "most blessed of women," her courage contrasting sharply with Sisera's mother, who vainly awaited her son's return.

The closing prayer summarizes the lesson: "So may all your enemies perish, O LORD! But your friends be like the sun as he rises in his might." Faith-filled courage shines like the morning light—it blesses others and glorifies God.

5. The legacy of leadership and obedience

Judges 5 ends with forty years of peace, the fruit of courageous obedience. Yet the peace came not from human strategy but from divine power working through faithful servants. Deborah's leadership, Barak's obedience, and Jael's courage formed a portrait of God's partnership with his people. When fear gives way to faith, God does great things through ordinary lives.

APPLICATION

1. Courageous leadership begins with trust in God's Word

Deborah's strength came not from position or personality but conviction. She believed what God said and acted upon it. True leadership always begins with trust in God's promises. In times of moral confusion, courageous Christians listen for his voice and speak his truth. Fear often paralyzes those who rely on human approval, but faith propels those who rely on divine authority. Our homes, churches, and communities need men and women who, like Deborah, lead by faith, not fear. The greatest influence we can offer others is the steady example of obedience rooted in God's Word.

2. Obedience turns fear into strength

Barak's story teaches that obedience transforms hesitation into confidence. At first, he feared the chariots of iron, but when he acted on God's command, his courage grew. Faith is not a feeling—it is a decision to trust God enough to act. Many Christians wait to feel brave before obeying, but Scripture calls us to obey first and discover courage along the way. The Lord often works through reluctant hearts that finally step forward. Once we move, he multiplies our strength and confirms his promise. Spiritual growth always follows obedient action.

3. Worship is the proper response to victory

The "Song of Deborah" teaches that gratitude completes obedience. God's people must not only fight in faith but sing in thanksgiving. Worship turns private courage into public testimony. When we celebrate what God has done, we encourage others to trust him. The song rebuked the complacent tribes and exalted the willing ones, reminding us that true worship includes both praise and challenge. Every act of deliverance deserves a song of praise, and every faithful victory should drive us to deeper devotion. God's glory must be the final word in all our successes.

CONCLUSION

Deborah, Barak, and Jael showed that faith is not the absence of fear but the courage to act on God's word despite it. Through their obedience, God transformed weakness into victory and proved that his power works through those who trust him completely. Their story called Israel—and us—to respond to God's promises with bold faith rather than hesitation.

Yet even as peace followed their triumph, Israel's devotion would again fade. Lesson 4 turns to Gideon, a reluctant man called in fearful times. His story will reveal how God meets insecurity with assurance, tests faith through obedience, and clothes the timid with his Spirit. The same God who honored Deborah's courage will now shape Gideon's weakness into strength.

REFLECTION

1. Why did God raise Deborah during Israel's oppression?
2. How did Deborah's faith inspire Barak's obedience?
3. What role did God play in Israel's victory?
4. How does Jael's act fulfill Deborah's prophecy?
5. What lessons emerge from the Song of Deborah?

DISCUSSION

1. What does courageous leadership look like today?
2. How can obedience replace fear in your faith?
3. Why must victories end in worship, not pride?
4. What "iron chariots" challenge your obedience?
5. How can your leadership inspire others' faith?

4

THE CRISIS OF FAITH

JUDGES 6

Objective: To recognize how God met Gideon's weakness with grace and transformed doubt into faith.

INTRODUCTION

When Israel once again fell into idolatry, God allowed the Midianites to oppress them until their cries reached heaven. The nation that once marched boldly under Joshua now hid in caves and threshed grain in secret. Into this fearful setting, God called a reluctant man named Gideon. His story reveals that the Lord does not choose servants because they are fearless but because he intends to make them faithful. Gideon's journey from doubt to devotion illustrates how divine grace patiently shapes human weakness into strength.

Gideon began as a man hiding from his enemies, questioning God's presence and doubting his own worth. Yet through each encounter—the angel's message, the destruction of Baal's altar, the filling of God's Spirit, and even the signs of the fleece—God patiently transformed a trembling heart into a trusting one. Every step of obedience deepened Gideon's confidence not in himself, but in the God who promised, "I will be with you."

This lesson reminds us that faith rarely begins fearless. It grows as God meets us in our hesitation, proves his faithfulness, and calls us forward.

EXAMINATION

1. Israel's misery under Midian (6:1-6)

Israel once again "did evil in the sight of the LORD," and God delivered them into the hands of Midian for seven years. The oppression was severe. Midianite raiders, joined by Amalekites and other eastern tribes, swept through the land like locusts, consuming every resource. Israel's economy collapsed, and the people fled to the hills. The text vividly depicts a nation stripped of dignity and provision. Their suffering was not random; it was divine discipline designed to bring repentance. The Lord often allows external pressure to expose internal corruption. When human strength fails, hearts became open to grace.

2. The prophet's rebuke (6:7-10)

When Israel cried out, God's first response was not a deliverer but a prophet. His message recalled God's past deliverance from Egypt and his covenant commands. The problem lay not in God's faithfulness but in Israel's forgetfulness. They had feared other gods and forfeited divine protection. The prophetic word reminded them that repentance must precede rescue. God desired transformation, not just relief. Before he sent a warrior, he sent his word.

3. God's call to Gideon (6:11-24)

The Angel of the Lord appeared under an oak in Ophrah, where Gideon secretly threshed wheat in a winepress to hide it from Midian. The setting captures the nation's fear: even its potential deliverer worked in hiding. The angel greeted him, "The LORD is with you, O mighty man of valor." The title sounded ironic; Gideon was anything but courageous. Yet God's address revealed divine perspective—he spoke to Gideon not as he was but as he would become by grace.

Gideon's response was filled with complaint: if God was truly with them, why had all this happened? Where were His miracles? The Lord answered, "Go in this might of yours." reminding Gideon that divine power works through available weakness. Still, Gideon doubted his worth, claiming his clan was the least in Manasseh and he the least in his family. God replied simply, "I will be with you." That assurance turned weakness into possibility.

To confirm the call, Gideon offered a meal of meat and bread. The angel touched it with his staff, and fire consumed it. Suddenly, Gideon realized he had encountered the Lord himself. Terrified, he feared death, but God spoke peace: "Do not fear; you shall not die." Gideon built an altar and named it Yahweh-Shalom—"The LORD is Peace." In the midst of fear, God gave assurance.

4. Tearing down Baal's altar (6:25-32)

Before leading the nation, Gideon had to cleanse his own household. That night, God commanded him to destroy his father's altar to Baal and cut down the Asherah pole beside it. In its place, he was to build an altar to the Lord and offer a bull as sacrifice. Gideon obeyed, but he did it under cover of darkness, afraid of his family and townspeople. Fear did not disqualify him; obedience amid fear defined him.

When morning came and the people discovered what had happened, they demanded Gideon's death. But his father, Joash, defended him: "If [Baal] is a god, let him contend for himself." Joash's words exposed the impotence of idols. The altar of Baal fell, and the God of Israel reasserted his rightful place in Ophrah. Gideon's private act of obedience became a public witness to divine authority.

5. God's Spirit empowered Gideon (6:33-35)

Soon after, the Midianites and their allies gathered in the valley of Jezreel. At that moment, "the Spirit of the LORD clothed Gideon." The phrase suggests divine possession—Gideon became God's instrument, wrapped in his power. He sounded the trumpet, and the tribes of Manasseh, Asher, Zebulun, and Naphtali rallied behind him. The fearful farmer became a Spirit-filled leader. What human resolve could not achieve, divine empowerment accomplished.

6. The fleece of reassurance (6:36-40)

Yet even after experiencing God's power, Gideon still wrestled with doubt. He asked for a sign: that dew would fall on the fleece but not the ground, and then the reverse. Both tests were granted. The text did not commend Gideon's request as a model of faith but revealed God's patience with frail believers. The Lord condescended to strengthen Gideon's wavering trust rather than rebuke him. The story ends with Gideon ready to lead, not because fear had vanished but because faith had matured through grace.

7. The theological pattern

Judges 6 portrays a God who confronted sin, called the unqualified, purified the fearful, and empowered the obedient. Gideon's story is not about human heroism but divine patience. The Lord's strength clothed a trembling man and turned him into a deliverer. The chapter taught that God meets doubters not with condemnation but with commissioning.

APPLICATION

1. God's call meets us in weakness

Gideon's story reminds believers that God often chooses those least likely to succeed. He found Gideon hiding, not conquering. Yet God saw potential where Gideon saw inadequacy. The call to serve always begins with God's initiative, not human confidence. When we feel unqualified, we are precisely where grace works best. The Lord still calls ordinary people to extraordinary tasks, not because of their strength but because his presence transforms fear into faith. Our hiding places can become holy places when God meets us there.

2. Obedience must begin at home

Before Gideon could confront Midian, he had to confront idolatry in his own household. True reform starts privately before it becomes public. God still asks his servants to tear down the altars of compromise closest to them—habits, attitudes, or loyalties that rival his rule. Gideon obeyed at night, yet God accepted his trembling obedience. The issue was not how boldly he acted but that he acted at all. Small steps of faith often ignite large movements of renewal.

3. God's patience nurtures growing faith

Gideon's repeated need for reassurance illustrates God's remarkable patience. The Lord did not despise his weakness but worked through it. Many believers carry guilt over imperfect faith, but God delights in shaping trust gradually. He did not scold Gideon for the fleece; he strengthened him through it. The Lord understands our frailty and meets us with gentle persistence. The God who clothed Gideon with his Spirit still empowers hesitant hearts today. When we bring our fears honestly before him, he responds not with rejection but with reassurance.

CONCLUSION

Gideon's story reveals a God who met fear with patience, doubt with assurance, and weakness with power. The Lord did not demand instant confidence but nurtured faith step by step, transforming a hesitant farmer into a courageous leader. Yet even as God strengthened Gideon, the lesson warns that faith must remain humble. The same God who empowers his servants also tests their dependence, ensuring glory belongs to him alone.

In the next lesson, we will see how that test unfolded. Gideon's faith brought stunning victory over Midian, but his success exposed a new danger—the pride that follows triumph. Lesson 5 will show how spiritual victory can quickly become spiritual vulnerability when devotion gives way to self-reliance and gratitude fades into glory-seeking.

REFLECTION

1. What caused Israel's oppression under Midian?
2. Why did God send a prophet before a deliverer?
3. How did God's greeting to Gideon reveal grace?
4. What did Gideon's obedience at night demonstrate?
5. How did the fleece reveal both weakness and mercy?

DISCUSSION

1. Where has God met you in weakness?
2. What "altar" might he ask you to tear down?
3. How has God strengthened your faith through patience?
4. Why is obedience amid fear still valuable?
5. How can Gideon's story encourage hesitant believers today?

5

GIDEON'S TRIUMPH & TRAGEDY

JUDGES 7-8

Objective: To learn that humility sustains victory while pride destroys what faith has achieved.

INTRODUCTION

The story of Gideon reaches its dramatic climax in these chapters, where faith and failure stood side by side. God granted Israel victory not through power, strategy, or numbers, but through weakness surrendered to his will. A trembling farmer led a band of three hundred men against a vast army, armed not with weapons but with faith. Their triumph declared one truth: God alone delivers his people, and he often does so through the least likely instruments. The same Gideon who once hid in fear became the vessel through which God's strength shone most clearly.

Yet the story did not end in triumph. Success introduces new temptations—self-reliance, vengeance, and pride. The man who tore down idols later built one; the leader who refused kingship in word lived like a king in deed. Gideon's life warned that the battle against pride can be harder than the battle against enemies. Victory gained through faith can quickly be lost through arrogance.

This lesson reminds us that humility sustains what faith begins. The

God who grants victory through weakness also demands worship beyond the battlefield.

EXAMINATION

1. God reduced the army (7:1-8)

At the spring of Harod, Gideon faced a vast Midianite host spread across the valley "like locusts in abundance." Israel's thirty-two thousand troops already felt inadequate, yet God declared, "The people with you are too many for me to give the Midianites into their hand." The problem was pride, not numbers. If Israel claimed credit, the glory due to God would vanish.

The first reduction was voluntary: those who were fearful could return home. Twenty-two thousand departed, leaving ten thousand. God said, "The people are still too many." At the water's edge, he tested them again. Only those who lapped water with their hands remained—three hundred men. God had whittled the army to less than one percent of its original size. Human probability had disappeared so that divine certainty could shine.

The reduction taught a timeless truth: dependence is the prerequisite for deliverance. Faith often begins where self-reliance ends. The fewer the soldiers, the greater the opportunity for God to reveal his power.

2. God reassured Gideon through a dream (7:9-15)

That night God spoke again: "Arise, go down against the camp, for I have given it into your hand." Yet he knew his servant's heart and added, "But if you are afraid to go down, go down to the camp with Purah your servant." Gideon obeyed quietly and listened from the shadows.

In one tent, a Midianite told his comrade, "Behold, I dreamed a dream, and behold, a cake of barley bread tumbled into the camp of Midian and came to the tent and struck it so that it fell." Barley bread, the food of the poor, symbolized Israel's weakness. His comrade answered, "This is no other than the sword of Gideon. ... God has given into his hand Midian" The humble loaf had become a prophetic picture of divine victory.

When Gideon heard the interpretation, he bowed in worship. Courage returned, not because the odds changed, but because God's word had been confirmed. Fear yielded to faith the moment Gideon remembered whose battle this truly was.

3. God gave victory through weakness (7:16-25)

Gideon divided his three hundred into three companies. Each man carried a trumpet, an empty jar, and a torch hidden inside. No swords, no spears—only light and sound in trembling hands. At the beginning of the middle watch, they encircled the camp. Gideon cried, "Do as I do."

At his signal they broke the jars, raised the torches, blew the trumpets, and shouted, "A sword for the LORD and for Gideon!" Chaos erupted. The Lord himself threw the Midianites into confusion so that they turned their swords on one another. Panic rippled through the valley as the once-invincible army fled toward the Jordan. Israel pursued, and reinforcements from Naphtali, Asher, and Ephraim joined the chase, capturing the leaders Oreb and Zeeb.

The entire episode reversed military logic. Israel's torches, trumpets, and shouts symbolized testimony rather than might. God saved by spectacle of faith, not strategy of force. The shattering jars prefigured hearts broken of self-trust so that divine light could shine. Victory belonged wholly to the Lord.

4. Gideon's zeal turned into vengeance (8:1-21)

When Gideon pursued the retreating kings, cracks began to show in his spirit. The Ephraimites complained that he had not summoned them sooner. Once gentle, Gideon pacified them diplomatically, saying, "What have I done now in comparison with you?" His humility, however, proved short-lived.

Crossing the Jordan, Gideon's weary men begged for bread from the leaders of Succoth and Penuel. Both towns refused, fearing Midian's reprisal. Gideon swore retribution. After capturing Zebah and Zalmunna, the Midianite kings, he did exactly that—tearing down Penuel's tower and flogging the elders of Succoth with thorns. What began as zeal for God's cause had become personal vengeance.

Gideon interrogated the captured kings and executed them himself, avenging the death of his brothers slain at Tabor. His actions blurred the line between righteous justice and private revenge. The servant who once trembled before enemies now lorded power over allies. Spiritual victory on the battlefield had turned into moral defeat in the aftermath.

5. Gideon's dangerous success (8:22-27)

When the fighting ceased, gratitude filled the nation. The people said, "Rule over us, you and your son and your grandson also." Outwardly Gideon refused: "I will not rule over you, and my son will not rule over you; the LORD will rule over you." The confession sounded pious, but his next request betrayed another motive. He asked for gold earrings from the plunder—seventeen hundred shekels in total—and fashioned them into an ephod, a sacred garment like the high priest's.

Perhaps he intended the ephod as a memorial to God's victory, but his creation soon became an idol. "All Israel whored after it there, and it became a snare to Gideon and to his family." The man who once destroyed his father's idol now made one of his own. Prosperity succeeded where persecution had failed. The external enemies had fallen; the internal enemy of pride had risen.

6. Gideon's family and legacy (8:28-32)

The land rested forty years under Gideon's leadership—the final season of rest recorded in Judges. Yet peace proved superficial. Gideon lived like a monarch, maintaining a large household and many wives. One son he named Abimelech, meaning "my father is king." The irony was devastating: the judge who verbally denied kingship symbolically claimed it through his son's name.

When Gideon died, Israel reverted quickly to Baal worship and forgot the Lord who had delivered them. The cycle began again. The tragedy was not only Gideon's decline but the spiritual vacuum he left behind. His ephod and his pride ensured that the peace he won would not endure beyond his lifetime.

7. The theological message

Judges 7-8 portray two sides of one man and one principle. Gideon's faith displayed God's strength through weakness; Gideon's pride displayed human weakness through success. The same Spirit who empowered him for battle could not force humility upon a heart unguarded by gratitude. The lesson extended beyond Gideon: every believer faces the same tension between dependence and self-confidence. The God who wins victories through us also tests whether we will keep them by worshiping him alone.

APPLICATION

1. Strength through dependence, not numbers

God reduced Gideon's army until no one could mistake the source of deliverance. The smaller the army, the larger the glory. Our instinct seeks security in size—resources, credentials, approval—but God delights in overturning those calculations. When he diminishes our self-reliance, he is not weakening us but preparing us for his power. The church's greatest victories have rarely come from abundance but from surrender. Gideon's torch-lit night reminds us that faith, not force, conquers the impossible. In seasons when we feel outnumbered, we stand on the edge of divine demonstration.

2. Victory demands faith before, humility after

Gideon's fall warns that triumph can intoxicate. Before battle he feared; after battle he forgot. Pride quietly replaced dependence until he mirrored the very arrogance God had judged in others. True faith must survive not only the test of crisis but the test of comfort. Humility is the discipline that keeps memory sharp—remembering who won the battle, who gave the resources, and who deserves the credit. Every answered prayer, every ministry success, every restored relationship must end with praise that protects the heart from pride.

3. Finishing well requires constant worship and obedience

The book of Judges closes each cycle with the same pattern: momentary faith followed by long forgetfulness. Gideon's ephod symbolized good intentions corrupted by idolatry. He wanted to commemorate victory but instead created a counterfeit religion. Finishing well means keeping eyes fixed on the Lord long after the trumpets fade. We finish faithfully not by doing something new but by continuing what once brought victory—trusting, worshiping, and obeying the same God who first delivered us. Persevering gratitude becomes the safeguard of legacy.

CONCLUSION

Gideon's rise and fall reminded Israel—and us—that victory belongs to God alone. The same Lord who granted triumph through weakness deserved all glory afterward. Yet Gideon's heart drifted from dependence to pride, turning success into stumbling. His story reveals that humility sustains faith, but self-reliance corrupts it. The torch that once shone with God's light dimmed when its bearer sought his own.

As the nation enjoyed temporary peace, the seeds of rebellion were already taking root. Lesson 6 will show how Gideon's legacy of compromise ripened into tragedy through his son Abimelech. Israel's first taste of human kingship exposed the danger of exalting self above God—a warning that true leadership must be grounded in faith, gratitude, and obedience, not ambition or pride.

REFLECTION

1. Why did God insist on reducing Gideon's army?
2. How did the barley-bread dream strengthen Gideon's faith?
3. What did Gideon's pursuit reveal about his heart?
4. Why was the ephod spiritually dangerous?
5. How did Gideon's legacy affect Israel's future?

DISCUSSION

1. When has weakness increased your dependence on God?
2. How can humility guard success in life and ministry?
3. What practices keep gratitude alive after triumphs?
4. Why is finishing well harder than starting strong?
5. How will you ensure victory leads to worship, not pride?

6

THE PERIL OF SELF-EXALTATION

JUDGES 9

Objective: To understand how pride and self-exaltation brought ruin to Abimelech and those who followed him.

INTRODUCTION

The story of Abimelech stands as one of the darkest episodes in the book of Judges. What began as Gideon's legacy of victory turned into a tale of unchecked ambition and ruin. After his father's death, Abimelech sought not to serve God's people but to rule them. His pursuit of power was born not from calling but from pride. By murdering his brothers and manipulating his relatives, he seized a throne that God never offered. His reign, built on blood and flattery, became a monument to the truth that ambition without submission always leads to destruction.

Abimelech's rise revealed how far Israel had drifted from covenant faithfulness. The people who once cried to God for deliverance now crowned a murderer financed by idol worship. Yet even in judgment, God remained sovereign. The same Lord who had delivered his people through Gideon would now discipline them through Abimelech's downfall.

This lesson challenges us to see that leadership divorced from humility becomes tyranny, and that self-exaltation always ends in humiliation. Pride not only destroys the arrogant but also those who follow them blindly.

EXAMINATION

1. Abimelech's ruthless rise (9:1-6)

After Gideon's death, Israel again drifted into idolatry. Amid this spiritual confusion, Abimelech, Gideon's son by a concubine in Shechem, conspired to make himself king. He went to his mother's relatives, saying, "Remember … that I am your bone and your flesh." He flattered them with family loyalty, turning kinship into a political weapon. They gave him seventy shekels of silver from the temple of Baal-berith—blood money dedicated to a false god—and Abimelech hired "worthless and reckless fellows" as his followers.

Together they went to Ophrah, Gideon's hometown, and slaughtered his seventy brothers on one stone. The act was as deliberate as it was brutal—an imitation of pagan enthronement rituals that required sacrifice. Only the youngest son, Jotham, escaped. Abimelech was crowned king by the oak of Shechem, near the very tree where God had once confirmed his covenant with Abraham. The contrast was horrifying: what began as a place of promise became a place of perjury. Leadership born in murder bore the seeds of its own destruction.

2. Jotham's prophetic fable (9:7-21)

When Jotham heard of Abimelech's coronation, he climbed Mount Gerizim overlooking Shechem and cried out his parable—the oldest recorded fable in Scripture. It was both satire and sermon.

He told of trees seeking a king. The olive tree, the fig tree, and the vine each refused the crown, content to serve by producing oil, fruit, and wine. Only the bramble, worthless and combustible, accepted the offer, promising shade it could not give and threatening to consume with fire those who resisted. The message was unmistakable: noble men decline self-glory to continue their service; worthless men grasp it and destroy.

Jotham declared that if Shechem had acted in good faith, let them rejoice in Abimelech; but if not, "let fire come out from Abimelech and devour the leaders of Shechem … and let fire come out from the leaders of Shechem … and devour Abimelech." He fled immediately, for his words were more than a warning—they were a prophecy. God had already begun to write the sentence of judgment.

The fable exposed a fundamental truth about leadership: power that seeks its own honor consumes both ruler and ruled. When people exchange faithfulness for flattery, they enthrone the bramble.

3. God sends discord as judgment (9:22-25)

For three years Abimelech ruled over Israel, or more precisely over Shechem, since his reign never extended nationally. His throne was an illusion maintained by fear. Then the Lord intervened: "God sent an evil spirit between Abimelech and the leaders of Shechem." This phrase does not mean God created evil but that he allowed hostility to expose the corruption both had sown. As Gideon's son had betrayed his brothers, so his followers would betray him.

Shechem's leaders grew restless under tyranny and conspired to ambush travelers loyal to Abimelech, weakening his support. The unrest that followed was not random chaos—it was divine justice unraveling evil from within. When God judges arrogance, he often lets pride become its own punishment. Abimelech's kingdom began to crumble as surely as the stone where his brothers had died.

4. The rebellion of Gaal (9:26-41)

A new character enters the story: Gaal son of Ebed, a swaggering opportunist who stirred Shechem's discontent. During a drunken festival in the temple of Baal-berith, he mocked Abimelech and boasted that if he were ruler, he would overthrow him. The crowd cheered his arrogance. Zebul, the city's governor and Abimelech's ally, secretly warned the king.

At night, Abimelech laid an ambush. When morning came, Gaal saw troops descending from the hills. Zebul taunted him, saying, "Where is your mouth now?" Gaal fought but fled, and Abimelech drove him out. Shechem's rebellion failed, yet the city's guilt remained. The stage was set for judgment. The very people who had funded Abimelech's violence now reaped its reward.

5. The destruction of Shechem (9:42-49)

The next day, the people of Shechem went out to the fields, perhaps thinking the danger had passed. Abimelech attacked again, divided his men into companies, and slaughtered them. He captured the city, killed its inhabitants, and razed it to the ground. To mark its curse, he scattered salt over the ruins—a symbolic act declaring permanent desolation.

Some citizens fled to the temple tower of El-berith, seeking sanctuary in the very idol's shrine whose treasury had financed their king's crimes. Abimelech ordered his men to gather branches, pile them against the tower, and set it ablaze. About a thousand men and women perished. The fire that Jotham foretold had begun to consume both the bramble and those who crowned it. Divine retribution was unfolding exactly as predicted.

6. Abimelech's death and divine justice (9:50-57)

Abimelech pressed on to Thebez, another nearby city, perhaps seeking to extinguish every remnant of opposition. The citizens retreated to a strong tower in the center of the city. As Abimelech approached to burn it down, a woman dropped an upper millstone from the wall, crushing his skull. Mortally wounded, he commanded his armor-bearer, "Draw your sword and kill me, lest they say of me, 'A woman killed him.'" Even in death, pride governed him.

The narrative concludes with theological clarity: "Thus God returned the evil of Abimelech, which he committed against his father in killing his seventy brothers. And God also made all the evil of the men of Shechem return on their heads." The story that began with ambition ended in irony—a bramble consumed by its own fire.

Abimelech's death restored the moral balance of the book. Though divine justice sometimes appears delayed, it never fails. God remains sovereign even when his people are faithless and their leaders corrupt. The account stood as a living parable of Proverbs 16:18: "Pride goes before destruction, and a haughty spirit before a fall."

7. The theological meaning

Judges 9 demonstrates that evil eventually self-destructs. God did not need a new deliverer; he simply allowed sinners to undo themselves. Abimelech's ambition and Shechem's complicity formed a partnership of pride, and both perished under divine justice. The Lord remained faithful to his covenant even through judgment, preserving Israel from permanent ruin.

The story also bridges two truths: human freedom and divine

sovereignty. Abimelech chose violence; God used his choices to display justice. Every generation faces the same tension—whether to crown self as king or to submit to God as Lord. One path leads to fire; the other to peace.

APPLICATION

1. Pride still destroys those who refuse submission

Abimelech's hunger for power mirrored humanity's oldest sin—the desire to rule without God. He gained influence through manipulation and maintained it through fear, but the Lord dismantled both. Pride always promises control and delivers collapse. When ambition eclipses obedience, ministry becomes monarchy and calling becomes competition. God still humbles those who exalt themselves. Every Christian must guard against the subtle rise of self-importance, remembering that service, not status, marks greatness in God's kingdom. The crown of self-will burns hotter than any earthly fire.

2. Leadership divorced from character invites disaster

Abimelech's leadership was positional, not spiritual. He wore authority like armor but lacked integrity beneath it. The people of Shechem chose him because he was a relative, not because he was righteous. They preferred charisma to character and reaped chaos. The same danger threatens every community of faith that values talent above truth or success above submission. God calls his people to discernment—to choose leaders whose hearts bow before him. Where leadership seeks glory rather than God, both leader and followers fall together.

3. God's justice remains certain though delayed

For three years, Abimelech's reign appeared secure. Yet God was quietly at work, orchestrating judgment through natural means—discord, rebellion, and even a falling stone. Divine justice often moves slowly, not because God forgets, but because he allows sin to reach full exposure. The believer's task is to trust his timing. When wrong seems unpunished and arrogance unchallenged, we remember Abimelech: the millstone still falls, and God's justice still stands. His patience is mercy, but his holiness is never mocked.

CONCLUSION

Abimelech's life proves that ambition without submission always leads to ruin. He sought power apart from God, built his throne on pride and bloodshed, and died beneath the weight of his own arrogance. His rise revealed how easily people follow charisma over character; his fall reminded Israel that God's justice cannot be mocked. The bramble that promised shade brought only fire.

Yet even amid such destruction, God remained faithful. Through judgment, he preserved his covenant and prepared Israel for new deliverers. In the next lesson, we will see how the cycle continued—how Jephthah's story reflected a nation still repeating its folly. When faith becomes reckless and devotion shallow, victory gives way once again to tragedy and decline.

REFLECTION

1. How did Abimelech's rise differ from earlier judges?
2. What truth did Jotham's parable teach about leadership?
3. How did God use discord to bring justice?
4. Why was Shechem's destruction poetic justice?
5. What did Abimelech's death reveal about pride?

DISCUSSION

1. How can ambition become spiritual danger?
2. What qualities should mark godly leadership today?
3. How do we trust God's justice amid corruption?
4. Where might pride tempt you to self-rule?
5. How can humility protect your ministry or influence?

7

THE FOLLY OF RASH FAITH

JUDGES 10-12

Objective: To learn that genuine faith submits to God's will instead of trying to manipulate his favor.

INTRODUCTION

After Abimelech's violent ambition brought judgment on Israel, the nation enters another downward spiral. The brief peace under Tola and Jair masked a deeper problem—Israel's heart remained unchanged. The people still confused remorse with repentance. When distress came, they cried out to God, but their words lacked sincerity. They sought relief, not renewal. This shallow repentance set the stage for Jephthah, a man whose own impulsive faith mirrored his nation's spiritual condition.

Jephthah's story reveals both the mercy and the tragedy of God's dealings with flawed humanity. Though rejected by his family, he was chosen to lead Israel against its enemies. Yet his greatest battle was not with the Ammonites but with his own misunderstanding of God. His rash vow—made in an attempt to secure divine favor—turned victory into heartbreak. The man empowered by the Spirit tried to bargain with the very God who had already promised deliverance.

This lesson exposes the danger of impulsive religion—zeal without understanding, promises without prayer, faith without submission. God desires trust that rests in his grace, not vows that try to earn it.

EXAMINATION

1. Tola and Jair: Stability after chaos (10:1-5)

After Abimelech's self-made kingship collapsed, God granted Israel a reprieve through two lesser-known judges. Tola from Issachar judged for twenty-three years at Shamir in Ephraim. His name meant "worm," perhaps symbolizing humility. His leadership provided rest, not revolution.

He was followed by Jair the Gileadite, who led for twenty-two years. Jair had thirty sons who rode thirty donkeys and governed thirty towns in Gilead—symbols of wealth and influence. Their reigns lacked the drama of deliverance but displayed administrative steadiness. Yet beneath outward order, spiritual erosion continued. Prosperity without devotion always breeds complacency. These short notices serve as a calm before the storm, reminding readers that peaceful times often conceal moral decay.

2. Israel's deepest apostasy (10:6-9)

After Tola and Jair, Israel's faith collapsed entirely. The writer lists seven gods—those of Syria, Sidon, Moab, Ammon, and the Philistines, along with Baal and Ashtaroth—representing total assimilation. Israel no longer flirted with idolatry; it had embraced it. The Lord's anger burned, and he sold them into the hands of the Philistines and Ammonites.

The oppression was severe. Ammon crossed the Jordan and devastated Gilead, while the Philistines pressed from the west. For eighteen years, Israel groaned under double tyranny. The people finally cried out, confessing, "We have sinned against you, because we have forsaken our God and have served the Baals." Yet this confession was mechanical—a ritual of desperation rather than repentance. Their words reached heaven, but their hearts still clung to idols.

3. God's weary response and reluctant mercy (10:10-16)

God's answer startled them. "Did I not save you from the Egyptians and from the Amorites, from the Ammonites and from the Philistines? The Sidonians also, and the Amalekites and the Maonites. … Yet you have forsaken me and served other gods; therefore I will save you no more. Go and cry out to the gods whom you have chosen." Divine weariness replaced divine pity.

For the first time in Judges, God seemed to refuse rescue. His response was not cruelty but tough love. He desired repentance that removed idols, not just words that requested relief. Confronted by silence, Israel finally acted—they threw away their foreign gods and served the Lord. The text then says, "He could bear Israel's misery no longer" (10:16 NIV). That sentence summarizes grace. God's compassion outlasted their rebellion. Though his people deserved rejection, his heart moved toward mercy. The stage was set for another deliverer.

4. Jephthah's unlikely calling (11:1-11)

Jephthah's background was marked by rejection. He was the son of a prostitute, driven from home by his half-brothers who denied him inheritance. He fled to the land of Tob, where "worthless fellows" gathered around him—a gang of outcasts turned warriors. When the Ammonites attacked, Israel's elders remembered the exile they had despised. In desperation, they begged him to lead.

Jephthah agreed, but only on one condition: if the Lord granted victory, he would become their head. The elders swore before the Lord to confirm the covenant. Ironically, the people who once rejected him now entrusted him with national leadership. Yet even in his rise, the story felt hollow. The Spirit of the Lord was not yet mentioned; this was a political arrangement, not a spiritual renewal. God would use Jephthah, but he would not sanctify his motives.

5. Jephthah's diplomacy and faith in history (11:12-28)

Before attacking, Jephthah attempted diplomacy. He sent messengers to the Ammonite king, challenging his claim to Israel's land. In a detailed review of history, he argued that Israel had not seized Ammonite territory but Amorite land, which God had given them. His theology was accurate: "All that the LORD our God has dispossessed before us, we will possess."

However, Jephthah's faith seemed more historical than relational. He knew God's acts but did not seem to know God's heart. He used truth as a bargaining tool rather than a testimony of trust. The Ammonite king rejected his appeal, setting the stage for battle. The Spirit of the Lord then came upon Jephthah—not to endorse his perfection but to empower his task. Yet the next verses reveals how shallow Jephthah's understanding of grace truly was.

6. Jephthah's rash vow (11:29-40)

As Jephthah marched to war, "the Spirit of the LORD was upon him." Nevertheless, he tried to secure success through a vow: "If you give the Ammonites into my hands, whatever comes out of the door of my house to meet me … will be the LORD's, and I will sacrifice it as a burnt offering."

This promise revealed a tragic mixture of faith and folly. He believed God could deliver but assumed victory required a bargain. His vow reflected pagan thinking—attempting to manipulate divine favor through sacrifice. God's Spirit was already with him; his vow only displayed ignorance of grace.

The Lord granted victory, and Jephthah defeated Ammon decisively. But when he returned home, his only child—his daughter—came out dancing to greet him. The horror of his words struck him. "You have brought me very low," he cried. She accepted her fate with sorrowful faith, asking only two months to mourn her virginity. The text emphasizes her purity, not her death, yet Jephthah "did with her according to his vow." Whether she died or lived in lifelong dedication to God, the result was tragedy. Israel's deliverer became another source of grief.

Jephthah's vow illustrates the folly of rash faith—belief that trusts in words and rituals rather than in God's mercy. His devotion lacked discernment. What he intended as piety became presumption. True faith rests in God's promise; false zeal tries to manipulate it.

7. The conflict with Ephraim (12:1-7)

Pride soon followed tragedy. The men of Ephraim, offended that Jephthah had not summoned them to battle, threatened to burn his house. Their arrogance repeated the earlier dispute with Gideon, but this time the outcome was deadly. Jephthah's patience had evaporated.

War erupted between Gilead and Ephraim. As the Ephraimites tried to flee across the Jordan, Gileadite soldiers devised a test. They demanded fugitives pronounce the word *shibboleth*. Ephraimites, unable to pronounce it correctly, said *sibboleth* and were executed. Forty-two thousand fell. The irony was devastating: the man whose "word" destroyed his daughter now destroyed his countrymen with another word. Civil war replaced unity, and the judge who delivered Israel from foreign enemies slaughtered his own people. After six years, Jephthah died, leaving behind a legacy of grief.

8. The final minor judges (12:8-15)

After Jephthah came Ibzan of Bethlehem, Elon of Zebulun, and Abdon of Pirathon. Together they ruled thirty-one years. Each detail of their wealth—sons, daughters, donkeys—contrasted sharply with Jephthah's loneliness. Their stories seemed peaceful but hollow. The absence of divine commentary signaled spiritual stagnation. Israel's faith had cooled to indifference. The book's downward spiral continued; the people valued comfort more than covenant.

9. The theological pattern

Judges 10-12 exposes the decline of both nation and leadership. Israel's repentance was shallow, Jephthah's faith was reckless, and Ephraim's pride was suicidal. God's mercy endured but his people learned little. The pattern of sin and deliverance had now become sin and deterioration. By the end of the section, Israel no longer looked for God; they looked for leaders who would secure ease without holiness. The "folly of rash faith" describes not only Jephthah's vow but the entire nation's religious shallowness.

APPLICATION

1. God desires repentance, not manipulation

Israel's cry for help sounded pious but lacked sincerity. They wanted relief without repentance. When God withheld immediate rescue, they finally cast aside their idols, proving that confession must be followed by change. The same principle remains true for believers today. God cannot be manipulated by emotional words or desperate promises. He seeks hearts that turn from sin, not voices that bargain for comfort. Genuine repentance always replaces idols with obedience. Shallow religion wants blessings; true faith wants God.

2. Zeal without wisdom leads to destruction

Jephthah's vow demonstrated passion without discernment. He believed in God's power but misunderstood his grace. Many believers today repeat his mistake—offering rash commitments or extreme sacrifices to earn divine favor already secured in Christ. God desires thoughtful devotion, not impulsive gestures. Spiritual maturity listens before it speaks and trusts before it vows. Zeal rooted in ignorance can wound others and dishonor God. Faith must be informed by Scripture, guided by humility, and surrendered to the Spirit.

3. Pride divides what faith unites

Ephraim's arrogance ignited civil war and revealed how self-importance ruins unity. They demanded recognition instead of rejoicing in victory. Pride still fractures communities and churches when egos overshadow mission. Humility remains the essential posture of faithful service. The more God uses us, the more carefully we must deflect praise toward him. Jephthah's generation learned that self-glory always ends in loss. Only humility preserves peace.

CONCLUSION

Jephthah's life reminded Israel that faith without wisdom leads to tragedy. His story exposed the emptiness of shallow repentance and the danger of trying to manipulate God through vows and rituals. True faith listens, waits, and obeys; false zeal acts first and prays later. Israel's repeated cycle of sin and sorrow showed that external victories cannot heal internal rebellion. Only surrender can.

As Israel drifted once more toward apathy, God's mercy again took the initiative. Lesson 8 will introduce Samson, a deliverer set apart before birth yet undone by his own impulses. Through his strength and weakness, we will see how divine purpose persists even in human failure—and how consecration without obedience always ends in compromise and loss.

REFLECTION

1. What revealed that Israel's repentance was shallow?
2. How did God show both justice and mercy?
3. Why was Jephthah's vow spiritually misguided?
4. What irony linked Jephthah's vow and civil war?
5. How did later judges (Ibzan, Elon, and Abdon) reflect Israel's decline?

DISCUSSION

1. What idols tempt Christians to seek relief without repentance?
2. How can we prevent zeal from becoming rashness?
3. Why is humility essential in spiritual leadership?
4. How can faith listen before it speaks?
5. What steps lead from genuine repentance to lasting renewal?

8

CALLED BUT COMPROMISED
JUDGES 13-14

Objective: To recognize how divine calling requires disciplined faith, not indulgent compromise.

INTRODUCTION

By the time Samson was born, Israel had grown comfortable under Philistine rule. The people no longer cried out for deliverance, and their silence revealed a heart content with compromise. Yet God, rich in mercy, acted on his own initiative. He raised up a deliverer before the nation even recognized its need. Samson's story began with divine promise and supernatural strength—but it unfolded as a tragedy of self-indulgence and squandered potential.

Set apart from birth under a Nazirite vow, Samson was called to embody consecration and dependence on God. Instead, his life reflected carelessness toward holiness. Every gift—his strength, his calling, his Spirit-given power—was overshadowed by unrestrained desire. The same man who tore lions apart could not master his own impulses. Through him, God began to free Israel, but his victories were incomplete because his faith lacked discipline.

Samson's early years reveal that divine calling is no guarantee of spiritual maturity. God may empower a servant, but only obedience sustains usefulness. Strength without surrender becomes self-destruction.

EXAMINATION

1. Israel's apathy and God's initiative (13:1-5)

The Philistine domination lasted forty years—the longest oppression recorded in Judges. The absence of repentance signaled a nation content with assimilation. God's deliverance, therefore, began not in human desperation but in divine compassion. Even when his people no longer sought him, he sought them.

Manoah and his wife lived in Zorah. She was barren, and in that despair, the angel of the Lord appeared to her, declaring, "You shall conceive and bear a son." The angel prescribed a Nazirite vow before the boy's birth: no wine, no unclean food, and no razor on his head. Unlike temporary Nazirites such as those described in Numbers 6, Samson's vow would be lifelong. His consecration from the womb signified that God's plan preceded human participation. Deliverance would arise solely from divine initiative.

2. Manoah's doubt and his wife's faith (13:6-23)

Manoah's wife reported the vision to her husband, describing "a man of God came to me [whose] his appearance was like the appearance of the angel of God, very awesome." Manoah prayed for further instruction, and the angel appeared again—to the woman. This repetition highlights the Lord's regard for her faith. Manoah's requests seemed well-intentioned, yet they exposed anxiety rather than trust. He desired to know the "child's manner of life," but the angel simply reiterated the same commands, emphasizing obedience over explanation.

When Manoah offered hospitality, the angel refused food but invited a burnt offering to the Lord. As the flame rose, the angel ascended in it and disappeared. Fear seized Manoah: "We shall surely die, for we have seen God!" His wife's calm reply revealed deeper faith: "If the Lord had meant to kill us, he would not have accepted a burnt offering and grain offering from our hands, nor shown us all these things." Her reasoning reflected confidence rooted in grace. Faith discerned what fear could not—that God's revelation was a promise, not a threat.

The couple named their son Samson, meaning "little sun." The name suggested brightness and strength, but as the story unfolds, his light flickers between divine power and human darkness.

3. The Spirit's stirring and Samson's potential (13:24-25)

Samson grew, and "the LORD blessed him." Then, "the Spirit of the LORD began to stir him in Mahaneh-dan." The Hebrew term implies restless movement—like wind that cannot be contained. God's Spirit was already at work, preparing Samson for his role as deliverer. Yet unlike earlier judges, the Spirit's activity did not lead to national repentance or unified leadership. Instead, it remained confined to personal empowerment. Israel's apathy left Samson standing alone. The deliverer's strength would operate amid a spiritually indifferent people.

These verses carried both hope and warning. Divine empowerment cannot compensate for moral indifference. The Spirit could stir Samson, but it could not override his choices. God's gifts always invite stewardship, not indulgence.

4. Samson's compromise begins (14:1-4)

The next chapter opens with dissonance. "Samson went down to Timnah, and at Timnah he saw one of the daughters of the Philistines." The verbs revealed a spiritual descent as well as a geographical one. He returned home demanding, "Get her for me, for she is right in my eyes." His parents protested, asking whether he could not find a wife among God's people. But Samson's eyes governed his heart; desire replaced discernment.

The narrator added, "His father and mother did not know that it was from the LORD, for he was seeking an opportunity against the Philistines." This did not excuse Samson's sin but explained God's sovereignty. The Lord could use human folly to accomplish divine purpose. Samson's impulsive pursuit of forbidden love became the spark that ignited conflict with Israel's enemies. God's plans never sanctioned disobedience, yet His providence could redeem even rebellion.

5. The lion and the honey (14:5-9)

As Samson and his parents journeyed to Timnah, a young lion roared against him. "the Spirit of the LORD rushed upon him," and he tore the beast apart with his bare hands. The episode demonstrates supernatural strength, but Samson told no one. Later, when he passed the carcass again, bees had made a hive inside. He scooped honey from the corpse and ate it, sharing it secretly with his parents.

This small act revealed deep compromise. As a Nazirite, Samson was forbidden to touch dead bodies. Yet curiosity and appetite triumphed over consecration. He enjoyed sweetness drawn from defilement—a fitting symbol of his life. What should have repelled him attracted him; what should have set him apart now entangled him. The man set apart by God was already violating the vow that marked his calling.

6. The wedding and the riddle (14:10-18)

Samson's marriage feast in Timnah mirrored pagan custom. Surrounded by Philistines, he proposed a riddle drawn from his earlier sin: "Out of the eater came something to eat. Out of the strong came something sweet." The riddle concealed his secret with the lion. The men failed to solve it for three days. In frustration, they pressured his new wife to entice the answer from him or face destruction. She wept and accused him of not loving her. Finally, Samson yielded.

When the men solved the riddle, Samson's anger blazed. "If you had not plowed with my heifer," he said, "you would not have found out my riddle." The crude insult revealed contempt both for his wife and for the covenant he ignored. The Spirit of the Lord again came upon him—not to endorse his rage but to use it for divine judgment. He struck down thirty Philistines in Ashkelon, took their garments, and gave them as payment. Then he stormed home in fury, leaving his bride behind. His father-in-law later gave her to another man. Passion without restraint had already ruined his first relationship and stained his ministry.

7. The theological significance of Samson's early years

Samson's calling and compromise illustrated the tension between divine sovereignty and human responsibility. God's Spirit empowered him for deliverance, yet his appetites continually undermined his purpose. The angel's prophecy said he would "begin" to deliver Israel, implying his work would remain incomplete. His victories weakened Philistia but did not free Israel.

Samson's story anticipated a deeper deliverance still to come. Like

Israel, he was chosen but disobedient, blessed but blind to his calling. Yet God's faithfulness persisted. Even flawed instruments can advance divine plans, but they cannot substitute for obedience. Samson's early years warned that gifting without holiness leads to waste, and strength without surrender becomes self-destruction.

APPLICATION

1. God's grace works even when his people grow indifferent

Israel never cried out for help, yet God still acted. His compassion did not depend on human initiative. The angel's visit to Manoah's wife reminds us that grace often begins in silence, when faith seems extinct. God still intervenes when his people no longer deserve it. Believers can find hope that God's mercy precedes repentance—but also warning that apathy invites discipline. Gratitude for divine grace should stir renewed devotion, not complacency.

2. Calling demands consecration

Samson's Nazirite vow represented separation for God's purposes, but he treated it as a decoration rather than a devotion. Modern disciples face the same temptation—to cherish identity without practicing holiness. God's calling requires daily discipline: guarding the senses, governing desires, and submitting ambitions to his will. The Spirit may empower us for service, yet power without purity dishonors the One who gives it. Strength is safest in hands that stay surrendered.

3. Compromise begins subtly but ends destructively

Samson's downfall started not in Delilah's lap but in Timnah's vineyards. He tolerated small violations until sin no longer felt serious. Touching the carcass, tasting the honey, ignoring parental counsel—each step eroded his distinctiveness. Compromise often feels sweet at first; its bitterness follows later. The Christian who toys with temptation eventually finds strength drained and peace lost. Faithfulness requires vigilance even in minor choices.

4. God's sovereignty does not excuse disobedience

The narrator's statement that Samson's actions were "from the LORD" underscored divine control, not divine approval. God's providence can weave human failure into his plan, but that never lessens personal accountability. The believer cannot justify sin by appealing to God's sovereignty. The Lord may redeem our mistakes, yet he never condones them. Reverence demands obedience even when his purposes remain mysterious.

CONCLUSION

Samson's early life revealed the tragedy of wasted potential. Set apart from birth, he was called to display God's strength through holiness, yet he allowed appetite to rule his heart. Every act of disobedience—whether choosing forbidden love or touching what was unclean—diminished his consecration. His story warns that divine calling requires disciplined faith, not indulgent compromise. Strength without surrender always collapses beneath temptation.

Yet even in Samson's failure, God's faithfulness endured. The Spirit who stirred him would not abandon him, though discipline would follow. Lesson 9 will trace how Samson's unchecked desires led to his downfall—and how, through judgment, God brought restoration. In his weakness, we will see the power of repentance and the grace of a God who redeems even the fallen.

REFLECTION

1. What made Israel's condition unique under Philistine rule?
2. How did Manoah's wife display greater faith than her husband?
3. What did the Nazirite vow signify about Samson's calling?
4. How did Samson's first acts foreshadow later failures?
5. What does his story teach about grace and responsibility?

DISCUSSION

1. Where do believers today risk spiritual apathy like Israel?
2. How can we guard our calling through daily consecration?
3. What small compromises threaten our integrity?
4. How does God's sovereignty encourage humility, not license?
5. How can Samson's failures deepen our dependence on grace?

9

SET APART BUT SET ADRIFT
JUDGES 15-16

Objective: To learn how spiritual drift wastes God's calling and how repentance restores his power.

INTRODUCTION

Samson's story reaches its climax in a swirl of contradiction—supernatural strength bound to human weakness, divine calling wasted by carnal desire. Chosen before birth, consecrated by vow, and empowered by God's Spirit, Samson was meant to begin Israel's deliverance from Philistine oppression. Yet the man set apart for holiness lived driven by impulse. His victories were impressive but shallow, his strength miraculous but misused. Every triumph fed his ego until the one who conquered others became a captive to himself.

This lesson traces the unraveling of Samson's life—how spiritual drift led him from victory to vengeance, from consecration to corruption, from freedom to chains. But even in ruin, the grace of God remained. The same Lord who empowered his rise also orchestrated his restoration. When pride broke and repentance stirred, strength returned. His greatest victory came not through defiance but through surrender.

Samson's life stands as both warning and hope: warning that spiritual privilege can be squandered through self-indulgence, and hope that repentance can restore what sin destroys.

EXAMINATION

1. A cycle of vengeance (15:1-8)

Samson's troubles resumed with personal offense. After abandoning his Philistine bride in anger, he returned during harvest "to visit his wife with a young goat," a gesture of reconciliation. Her father refused him, explaining that she had been given to another man. Enraged, Samson declared, "This time I shall be innocent in regard to the Philistines."

He captured three hundred foxes, tied their tails in pairs with torches, and released them through Philistine fields, burning their grain, vineyards, and olive groves. His vengeance devastated their economy but did not free Israel; it merely escalated hostilities. The Philistines retaliated by burning the woman and her father. Samson struck back again, "hip and thigh with a great blow." The text reads like an endless echo of retribution. Violence begot violence, and Israel's deliverer became entangled in the same brutality as their oppressors.

Samson's strength was divine, but his motives were personal. Instead of crying to God for deliverance, he acted on impulse. His zeal lacked submission, and his victories lacked direction.

2. God's deliverer isolated (15:9-13)

The Philistines then invaded Judah to capture Samson. Ironically, three thousand men of Judah—Israelites themselves—came to bind him and hand him over. They said, "Do you not know that the Philistines are rulers over us?" Their words expose the nation's resignation. They preferred bondage to battle. Samson, the man set apart to deliver them, now stood betrayed by those he came to save.

He agreed to be bound, insisting that they not kill him themselves. Their ropes represented more than restraint—they symbolized Israel's surrender. When God's people made peace with oppression, their deliverer seemed dangerous to them. Spiritual apathy had become their captivity.

3. Victory by God's Spirit (15:14-20)

As the Philistines approached shouting triumphantly, "the Spirit of the LORD rushed upon him." The ropes melted from his arms like burned flax. Finding a fresh jawbone of a donkey, Samson struck down a thousand men. The weapon underscored God's pattern of using weakness for victory. The jawbone, like Gideon's torch or Shamgar's oxgoad, displayed divine strength through humble means.

After the battle, Samson sang, "With the jawbone of a donkey have I struck down a thousand men." His song credited himself, not God. Yet soon thirst humbled him. He cried, "You have granted this great salvation by the hand of your servant, and shall I now die of thirst?" God answered, splitting open a hollow place and bringing forth water. Samson named it En-hakkore—"spring of the caller." The moment captured both God's mercy and Samson's inconsistency: pride followed by desperation, boasting followed by need. The Spirit's strength remained, but the heart that received it still wavered between faith and self-importance.

4. Strength without purity (16:1-3)

Samson later went to Gaza, a key Philistine stronghold, and spent the night with a prostitute. News spread, and the Philistines lay in wait at the city gate. At midnight, Samson arose, tore the massive gates from their hinges, and carried them to the hill facing Hebron. The act displayed astonishing power but hollow purpose. It humiliated Gaza but achieved no deliverance. Samson had become a spectacle rather than a savior—using divine strength for personal exhibition.

His public triumph masked private defeat. Every victory without purity hardened his conscience and distanced him further from his calling. He could remove Gaza's gates but not the spiritual chains closing around his heart.

5. The surrender of strength (16:4-20)

Sometime later, Samson fell in love with a woman in the Valley of Sorek named Delilah. The Philistine rulers offered her eleven hundred pieces of silver each to discover the secret of his strength. Four times she pressed him; four times he lied—first with bowstrings, then ropes, then weaving his hair into a loom. Each deception ended with betrayal, yet Samson stayed. The repetition revealed his blindness before blindness ever struck his eyes.

At last, weary of her persistence, he revealed the truth: "A razor has never come upon my head, for I have been a Nazirite to God from my mother's womb. If my head is shaved, then my strength will leave me, and I shall become weak and be like any other man." He treated consecration as superstition, confusing symbol with substance. His strength lay not in hair but in holiness—the sign of his devotion to God. When Delilah cut his hair, the Lord departed from him, and Samson did not know it. He awoke thinking he could shake himself free as before, but spiritual power once lost could not be summoned by habit. The Philistines seized him, gouged out his eyes, and bound him in bronze chains. The man who toyed with temptation was now its prisoner.

6. The grinding wheel of grace (16:21-22)

Blinded and enslaved, Samson ground grain in Gaza—the city whose gates he once carried away. Yet amid humiliation, grace returned quietly: "The hair of his head began to grow again." The regrowth was not magic but metaphor—a sign that repentance had begun. The God who withdrew his presence did not withdraw his purpose. Brokenness became the soil of renewal.

Samson's blindness stripped away distraction. For the first time, he stopped fighting Philistines and started confronting himself. The grinding wheel turned daily, but God was shaping his heart more deeply than his muscles had ever flexed. Strength without surrender had failed; now surrender would restore strength.

7. Death and redemption (16:23-30)

The Philistine lords gathered in the temple of Dagon to celebrate Samson's capture. "Our god has given Samson our enemy into our hands," they shouted. They brought him out to entertain them—a trophy of defeated Israel and mocked deity. The scene reversed earlier victories: the deliverer now stood as spectacle, and pagan worship appeared triumphant.

Placed between two central pillars, Samson prayed, "O Lord God, please remember me and please strengthen me only this once, O God, that I may be avenged on the Philistines for my two eyes." His prayer still mingled revenge with faith, yet it reached heaven. Grasping the pillars, he said,

"Let me die with the Philistines." He pushed with all his might, and the temple collapsed. The text concluded, "So the dead whom he killed at his death were more than those whom he had killed during his life."

The final scene carried paradox. Samson's greatest victory came through surrender, not survival. His strength returned not through hair but through humility. In death, he achieved what pride had prevented in life—an act of faith that restored God's honor among the nations. Israel buried him between Zorah and Eshtaol, the same valley where his story began. The circle closed with grace.

8. The theological message

Samson's life summarized the story of Israel itself: chosen, empowered, and continually compromised. Like the nation, he was consecrated to God yet captivated by the world. His blindness mirrored theirs. Yet God's faithfulness endured. Even when his servant failed, his purposes moved forward. The Spirit who departed also returned to accomplish redemption through judgment.

The tragedy of Samson warns that spiritual privilege cannot substitute for obedience. Gifts without character become weapons of self-destruction. Yet his restoration reminds believers that failure is not final when repentance is real. The God who used a broken Samson still redeems broken lives for his glory.

APPLICATION

1. Strength without submission leads to bondage

Samson's power dazzled others but deceived him. He believed anointing guaranteed immunity. Many believers make the same mistake—mistaking success for approval. God's gifts are meant for service, not self-display. When we use them selfishly, strength becomes a snare. True power lies not in performance but in surrender. The Spirit fills only what is yielded. Samson's chains warned that independence from God is the surest path to slavery.

2. God's discipline aims at restoration, not rejection

Samson's imprisonment appeared final, yet God was not finished. The slow regrowth of hair symbolized divine patience. The Lord disciplines to awaken, not destroy. When we suffer consequences for sin, he still calls us to repentance. Like Samson at the mill, our lowest moments can become turning points of grace. Brokenness that bends toward God becomes the beginning of renewal.

3. Redemption begins with surrender

Samson's final prayer was imperfect but sincere. He no longer fought for pride or pleasure but for God's vindication. In death, he accomplished what his life had wasted. His story teaches that surrender, not strength, wins the greatest battles. When we finally admit helplessness, God's power returns. The cross of Christ fulfilled that pattern perfectly—victory through sacrifice, strength through surrender, glory through humility (Phil. 2:5-11). Every Christiam who dies to self shares in that triumph.

CONCLUSION

Samson's final moments revealed the mercy of a God who restores what pride destroys. Though his strength had been wasted through self-indulgence, repentance brought redemption. In death, Samson accomplished more for God's glory than he ever had in life. His story reminded Israel—and us—that God's power is not lost through failure but through refusal to return. The same grace that met Samson in the ruins still meets repentant hearts today.

Yet as Israel buried its broken judge, the nation itself sank deeper into spiritual decay. Lesson 10 will move from Samson's personal fall to Israel's collective corruption, where homemade religion replaced holy worship. Micah's shrine and Dan's idolatry will reveal how a nation without obedience soon lost all discernment.

REFLECTION

1. How did Samson's strength become his weakness?
2. What did Israel's betrayal reveal about their faith?
3. How did God's mercy appear in Samson's imprisonment?
4. Why was his final act both judgment and grace?
5. What parallels exist between Samson's death and Christ's sacrifice?

DISCUSSION

1. How can God's gifts become dangerous when misused?
2. What spiritual "ropes" keep believers from obedience?
3. How does repentance restore power in a fallen life?
4. Where might pride disguise itself as strength today?
5. How can Samson's end inspire renewed surrender to God?

10

THE CORRUPTION OF PRIVATE RELIGION

JUDGES 17-18

Objective: To see how self-made religion dishonors God and destroys communities.

INTRODUCTION

The final chapters of Judges mark a shift from national deliverance to national decay. The story of Samson ended with personal failure and redemption; now the narrative turns to Israel's collective corruption. Without leadership, the people no longer sought God's word as their authority. Instead, they shaped religion according to preference and convenience. The repeated refrain, "In those days there was no king in Israel; everyone did what was right in his own eyes," captured a generation that confused sincerity with truth.

This lesson exposes the danger of worship divorced from revelation. Micah's household shrine, the wandering Levite's compromise, and the tribe of Dan's idolatry reveal a nation that had traded obedience for innovation. Their religion still used God's name but ignored his word. Faith had become imitation—a form of worship that looked spiritual but was rooted in self-will. What began as private devotion soon corrupted an entire tribe, proving that personal disobedience never stays private for long.

When God's truth is neglected, imitation faith rises to take its place. The result is always the same—confusion, corruption, and collapse.

EXAMINATION

1. Micah's household religion (17:1-6)

The story begins in the hill country of Ephraim, near Shiloh where the true sanctuary stood. A man named Micah confessed to his mother that he had stolen eleven hundred shekels of silver from her. She responded with surprising piety, blessing him "by the LORD" and dedicating the silver to make an idol. Together they fashioned a carved image and a molded image—violating the second commandment given at Sinai.

Micah established a private shrine, complete with an ephod and household gods, and ordained one of his sons as priest. His home became a counterfeit temple. The writer inserts his refrain: "In those days there was no king in Israel; everyone did what was right in his own eyes." The absence of authority allowed sincerity to substitute for obedience. Micah believed he was honoring the Lord, yet his devotion ignored God's word.

The irony was painful. Israel's covenant law demanded one sanctuary and one priesthood, yet Micah built a replica for convenience. He wanted religion that comforted him without confronting him—a faith manageable within his home. His name, meaning "Who is like Yahweh?" became a contradiction. Micah did not reject God outright; he reinvented him in silver.

2. A wandering Levite and corrupted ministry (17:7-13)

Soon a young Levite from Bethlehem arrived, seeking employment. Levites were supposed to serve throughout Israel, teaching the law and assisting in the true sanctuary, but this man drifted like a freelancer. He embodied the spiritual aimlessness of the age—trained for holiness but motivated by opportunity.

Micah invited him to live in his house, offering ten shekels of silver a year, clothes, and food. The Levite agreed, becoming Micah's personal priest. Micah rejoiced, saying, "Now I know that the LORD will prosper me, because I have a Levite as priest." His words reveal the superstition underlying his faith. He treated the Levite as a spiritual charm, believing that God's favor could be bought through ritual rather than received through obedience.

The Levite, whose name later appears as Jonathan son of Gershom, a descendant of Moses, accepted the position without protest. His silence condemned him. He should have torn down the idols; instead, he served before them. When Christians lose conviction, idolatry flourishes.

3. The wandering tribe of Dan (18:1-6)

The narrative widens from one household to an entire tribe. The Danites, unable to conquer the territory allotted to them, sought a new home. Their failure traced back to unbelief. Rather than fight for God's promise, they looked for an easier inheritance. Their search for land mirrored Micah's search for religion—both pursued convenience over calling.

Five Danite scouts traveled north and lodged at Micah's house. Recognizing the Levite's voice, they questioned him and asked for divine counsel about their mission. The Levite replied, "Go in peace. The journey on which you go is under the eye of the LORD." His blessing sounded pious but lacked substance. He inquired of no oracle; he simply told them what they wanted to hear. His words revealed a ministry reduced to affirmation rather than revelation.

4. The conquest of Laish (18:7-27)

The scouts discovered Laish, a peaceful city in the far north. The inhabitants lived secure, distant from allies and unaware of danger. Returning home, the spies urged their tribe to attack. Six hundred Danite warriors set out, passing again through Micah's house. On the way, they stole his idols and persuaded the Levite to join them. They promised him a promotion: "Is it better for you to be priest to the house of one man, or to be priest to a tribe and clan in Israel?" Ambition triumphed over loyalty. The Levite gladly left, carrying Micah's gods in his arms.

When Micah realized what had happened, he chased them, crying, "You take my gods that I made and the priest, and go away, and what have I left?" The irony is tragic. The man who manufactured his deity now lamented its theft. Any god that can be carried away is not worth worshiping. The Danites mocked him and continued north.

They attacked Laish, slaughtering its inhabitants and burning the city. Then they rebuilt it, renaming it Dan. The tribe installed Micah's idol and the same Levite as priest. The closing verse records that his descendants served "until the day of the captivity of the land." What began as one man's private religion became institutional idolatry for generations. Micah's silver shrine outlived the tabernacle at Shiloh. False worship proved far more persistent than faithfulness.

5. The corruption of worship (18:30-31)

The story ends with two grim facts: first, that Jonathan the priest descended from Moses, not Aaron; second, that idolatry endured "as long as the house of God was at Shiloh." The comparison was deliberate. True worship and false worship coexisted side by side, and Israel seemed unable to tell the difference.

The priestly line that once received God's law now presided over idols. The covenant nation no longer asked, "What has God said?" but, "What do we prefer?" The author offered no commentary beyond his refrain: "There was no king in Israel." Spiritual anarchy had replaced the rule of God's word. The Lord's name was still invoked, but his authority was ignored.

This narrative illustrates how apostasy creeps in quietly. Israel's fall did not begin with rejection of Yahweh but with imitation of him. Micah's shrine looked sacred, his Levite sounded legitimate, and Dan's worship appeared nationalistic. Yet every layer of devotion hid disobedience. Private religion corrupted public faith.

6. The theological message

Judges 17-18 diagnoses the heart of Israel's decay: self-rule in the realm of faith. The people created a religion that used God's vocabulary while rejecting his voice. Micah's house, the Levite's greed, and Dan's conquest portrayed a nation reshaping theology to fit desire. The covenant once founded on revelation had devolved into religious relativism.

The story also reveals how sin spreads. Micah's private sin infected a tribe; the tribe's idolatry shaped a nation. Personal compromise always becomes communal corruption. The silence of priests, the ambition of leaders, and the ignorance of worshipers combined to produce counterfeit spirituality. The tragedy was not that Israel worshiped other gods but that it worshiped the true God in false ways.

APPLICATION

1. Worship must follow revelation, not imagination

Micah's religion looked sincere, but sincerity cannot sanctify disobedience. God had already revealed how he was to be worshiped. When people invent their own forms of devotion—selecting what comforts and discarding what convicts—they repeat Micah's error. Faith becomes idolatry whenever it ignores Scripture. Genuine worship begins not with creativity but with submission. The God who saves determines how he is served.

2. Fearful leaders enable deception

The Levite's silence betrayed his calling. He knew the law yet served idols for income and security. His compromise encouraged corruption far beyond Micah's house. Spiritual leaders today face similar temptations—to trade truth for acceptance, conviction for comfort. Faithful leadership and ministry requires courage to confront error even when it costs popularity. The Levite's story warns that neutrality in matters of truth is never harmless; it blesses what God condemns.

3. Private compromise breeds public corruption

Micah's household shrine seemed minor compared to national apostasy, but it became the seed of tribal idolatry. Sin seldom remains contained. What begins as private convenience often shapes communities and generations. The integrity of individual faith affects the health of collective worship. Personal holiness is not optional; it guards the purity of God's people. When believers tolerate small idols in their homes, they prepare larger ones for their children.

4. Spiritual confusion thrives when truth loses authority

The repeated refrain—"everyone did what was right in his own eyes"—summarizes the danger of moral relativism. When truth becomes subjective—when everyone has their own "truth"—every opinion claims divine approval. Israel's idols bore Yahweh's name, yet they mocked his character. The same distortion appears whenever culture dictates belief instead of

Scripture. The antidote is renewed submission to God's Word. Authority must return to revelation, or faith will dissolve into imitation.

CONCLUSION

Micah's household shrine and the tribe of Dan's idolatry reveal how far Israel had fallen when truth was abandoned. What began as private sin became public corruption, proving that imitation religion always replaces revelation when God's Word is ignored. The Levite's compromise and Dan's conquest showed that self-made faith may appear spiritual but only multiplies deception and division. When people create a god they can manage, they lose the God who can save.

Lesson 11 will expose the full collapse that followed—moral, social, and spiritual. In Gibeah's outrage and Israel's civil war, we will witness a nation reaping the fruit of its own rebellion. Yet even in that darkness, a faint light of grace will remain, reminding us that God's mercy outlasts human ruin.

REFLECTION

1. Why did Micah's religion seem sincere yet remain sinful?
2. How did the Levite's compromise deepen corruption?
3. What does the Danite conquest teach about misplaced ambition?
4. How does this story reflect Israel's national decay?
5. Why is obedience essential to true worship?

DISCUSSION

1. How does modern culture promote "private religion"?
2. What safeguards help believers remain faithful to Scripture?
3. How can leaders resist the pressure to please people?
4. In what ways can small compromises affect a church's influemce?
5. How can God's people restore truth-based worship today?

11

THE CHAOS OF SELF-RULE
JUDGES 19-21

Objective: To understand how moral anarchy and self-rule led Israel to ruin—and why only God's kingship restores order.

INTRODUCTION

The closing chapters of Judges depict Israel's complete collapse—spiritually, morally, and socially. What began with individual compromise in Micah's house now spread across the nation. With no king to restrain them and no truth to guide them, "everyone did what was right in his own eyes." Religion had already turned to imitation; now morality dissolved into chaos. The stories that follow are among the darkest in Scripture, not for their violence alone, but for their revelation of what happens when God's people abandon his authority.

In Gibeah, the cruelty of Sodom reappeared among the covenant people. A Levite's cowardice, a woman's suffering, and a tribe's corruption exposed a nation that no longer resembled the one God had redeemed. Outrage replaced repentance, and vengeance masqueraded as justice. Even Israel's attempts to correct evil only deepened the disorder. The book that began with conquest ends with confusion—an entire generation living without the rule of God's word.

Yet beneath the ruin runs a thread of mercy. God preserved a remnant and prepared the way for a true King who would bring lasting peace.

EXAMINATION

1. The outrage at Gibeah (19:1-30)

The story begins with another wandering Levite—echoing the corruption of the priest in Micah's house. He lived far from his duties and took a concubine from Bethlehem. When she was unfaithful and fled home, he followed to bring her back. His concern appeared noble, but his motives were selfish. After days of delay, he departed late, ignoring his servant's warning to stay in Jerusalem and choosing instead to spend the night in Gibeah, a Benjaminite city.

As evening fell, no one offered hospitality until an old man welcomed them. But the night turned horrific. Wicked men surrounded the house, demanding to abuse the Levite. The scene deliberately echoes Sodom in Genesis 19—proof that Israel had become as depraved as the nations once judged. The host offered his own daughter and the concubine instead. The Levite thrust the woman outside to save himself. She was violated all night and died at the doorway.

At dawn, the Levite found her body, saying coldly, "Get up; let us be going." Receiving no response, he placed her on his donkey, returned home, and cut her corpse into twelve pieces—sending them throughout Israel. The act was gruesome but effective. Shock rippled across the tribes. Yet even in outrage, hypocrisy prevailed. The man who sacrificed his concubine now portrayed himself as victim, not perpetrator. His letter to Israel omitted his own guilt, igniting fury without repentance. The nation demanded vengeance on Gibeah but never confessed its own corruption.

2. The civil war (20:1-48)

Representatives from all Israel gathered at Mizpah. The Levite recounted his version of events, inflaming righteous anger. The tribes united and demanded that Benjamin surrender the men of Gibeah. The Benjaminites refused, choosing clan loyalty over justice. The line between good and evil blurred—one tribe defended depravity, another sought revenge.

Israel inquired of the Lord, asking who should lead the attack. God answered, "Judah first," recalling earlier victories. But when they fought, Benjamin struck down twenty-two thousand Israelites. Shocked, they wept and sought the Lord again. He sent them back, and again they were defeated—eighteen thousand more fell. Only after a third inquiry, when they fasted, sacrificed, and truly sought God's direction, did he grant victory.

Benjamin's army, once arrogant, was destroyed. Only six hundred men fled to the wilderness of Rimmon. The battle that began in justice ended in slaughter. Israel's zeal became excessive, wiping out entire towns of Benjamin, including women and children. The tribes had defended morality by committing massacre. Sin had conquered both victim and avenger. The people mourned their near extinction of a brother tribe but could not see that vengeance apart from humility always leads to tragedy.

3. Regret and rashness (21:1-15)

The tribes then faced a new crisis: how to preserve Benjamin without breaking their own oaths. They had sworn not to give their daughters as wives to Benjamin, yet they could not bear to see a tribe vanish from Israel. Their solutions combined pragmatism and hypocrisy. They sought to fix sin with more sin.

First, they remembered that one city, Jabesh-gilead, had not joined the war. They massacred its inhabitants, sparing only four hundred virgins to supply wives for Benjamin's survivors. This act of "mercy" mingled obedience with cruelty. Later, when more wives were needed, they devised another scheme. During the annual festival at Shiloh, Benjaminite men were told to hide in vineyards and seize dancing women as their wives. The elders promised to appease the women's families afterward. The plan succeeded, but righteousness did not. Israel's final act in the book of Judges was human improvisation—moral confusion dressed as compassion. The tribes wept, yet their tears did not cleanse their corruption. They mourned consequences, not sin.

4. The silence of God

Throughout these chapters, God's voice was almost absent. He spoke only three brief times, permitting battle but offering no comfort or counsel. His silence reflected judgment. When a nation ignores his Word, he allows it to reap the fruit of its choices. The refrain "no king in Israel" meant more than the absence of monarchy; it meant the rejection of divine authority. The covenant people had replaced God's rule with moral autonomy, and the result was chaos.

The Levite's cowardice, Benjamin's defiance, and Israel's vengeful excess all stemmed from the same root—everyone doing what was right in his own eyes. When truth becomes subjective, sin multiplies, and justice becomes vengeance. Even attempts to repair evil without repentance only deepen the wound. The narrator closes the book with no resolution, no repentance, no revival—only exhaustion and moral emptiness.

5. The thread of mercy

Yet a faint light flickered within the darkness. God preserved Benjamin's six hundred survivors, maintaining the unity of the twelve tribes. His covenant could not be extinguished by human failure. The preservation of a remnant hinted that redemption would come, but not from within this broken system. Judges ended crying for a king—not a tyrant like Abimelech, but a righteous ruler who would bring justice and peace. The silence of God in these chapters became the stage upon which his coming word would shine brighter (1 Sam. 3). The hope of the covenant still survived beneath the rubble of rebellion.

6. The theological message

Judges 19-21 illustrates what life becomes when divine truth is replaced by personal preference. Israel's social collapse reflected spiritual anarchy. Family, priesthood, justice, and compassion all disintegrated because each person pursued private righteousness rather than God's standard. The book closed not with victory but with vacancy—the absence of godly leadership and the desperate need for redemption.

Yet behind the horror, the story pointed toward God's enduring grace. His patience with such depravity testifies to a mercy deeper than judgment. The chaos of Judges cried out for a king who would rule not by human sight but by divine wisdom. That longing found its answer centuries later in Christ, the true Judge and King who restores what self-rule destroys.

APPLICATION

1. Moral autonomy always leads to moral anarchy

The refrain "everyone did what was right in his own eyes" describes more than ancient history—it exposed the human condition. When people discard God's authority, each becomes their own lawgiver. The result is confusion in society, chaos in relationships, and hypocrisy in religion. Truth cannot be replaced by opinion without consequence. Christians today must resist the temptation to define right and wrong by feeling or culture. God's Word remains the only stable foundation for moral life.

2. Outrage without repentance changes nothing

Israel's fury over the Levite's concubine united the tribes in indignation but not in humility. They condemned sin in others while ignoring it in themselves. Modern outrage often functions the same way—loud but hollow. True reform begins not with public fury but private confession. God cannot heal a people who grieve evil's effects but not its cause. Repentance, not reaction, restores righteousness.

3. Zeal without wisdom destroys more than it defends

Israel's war against Benjamin began in justice but ended in vengeance. Their righteous anger degenerated into cruelty. The same danger confronts believers who fight moral battles without spiritual discernment. Zeal for truth must be governed by humility and compassion, or it becomes destructive. The Lord's work cannot be done by worldly means. Justice without grace repeats the violence it condemns.

4. Mercy without holiness perpetuates corruption

The final chapter showed Israel's sentimental efforts to repair Benjamin's loss through unholy solutions. Compassion detached from obedience never honors God. Genuine mercy seeks restoration through righteousness, not compromise. The gospel reveals mercy that satisfies holiness—the cross where justice and grace meet. Only such mercy can heal the chaos of self-rule.

5. God's silence is not abandonment but warning

Throughout these chapters, God spoke little because his people listened less. When conscience dulls and truth is ignored, divine silence becomes discipline. Yet even silence is mercy, calling hearts back to the Word they have neglected. The absence of revelation drives us to seek the God who alone can speak order into confusion. When his people return in humility, the silence ends in grace.

CONCLUSION

The final chapters of Judges reveal what happens when truth vanishes and every heart becomes its own authority. Israel's descent into violence, idolatry, and moral anarchy show that self-rule always ends in ruin. The Levite's cruelty, Benjamin's defiance, and Israel's vengeance all testify to a nation without God's king and without God's Word. Yet even in silence, divine mercy endured—preserving a remnant and pointing forward to hope beyond the chaos.

Lesson 12 will carry the story to its theological summit. We will review the entire book of Judges to see its pattern of rebellion and redemption and how it ultimately prepared Israel—and us—for a righteous King whose rule alone can transform chaos into peace and failure into faith.

REFLECTION

1. How did Israel's sin in Gibeah resemble Sodom's?
2. What did the civil war reveal about Israel's heart?
3. Why was God largely silent in these chapters?
4. How did Israel's "solutions" expose further confusion?
5. What hope remained at the book's end?

DISCUSSION

1. How does moral relativism still corrupt faith today?
2. Why is repentance deeper than outrage?
3. How can zeal for truth remain humble and compassionate?
4. What lessons emerge from God's silence in Judges?
5. How does Christ answer the chaos described in this story?

12

NO KING BUT GOD

Objective: To understand that peace and purpose come only when God reigns as King over his people.

INTRODUCTION

The book of Judges ends not with triumph but with tragedy. What began with promise in the days after Joshua descended into chaos as "everyone did what was right in his own eyes." Across thirteen judges and multiple generations, the same pattern repeated—sin, oppression, repentance, deliverance, and relapse. Israel's story became a mirror of the human heart: resistant to God's authority yet desperate for his rescue. Each deliverer provided temporary relief, but none could bring lasting peace. The tragedy of self-rule revealed the necessity of God's rule.

Throughout the book, God's faithfulness stands in sharp contrast to Israel's failure. He raised up Othniel, Deborah, Gideon, and Samson to deliver his people, yet every victory faded into another fall. The problem was not political weakness but spiritual rebellion. Without God's kingship, freedom became bondage and worship turned into idolatry. Judges proved that human effort cannot sustain righteousness—only divine reign can restore order.

This lesson looks back across the entire book to see its message clearly: humanity cannot rule itself without destroying itself. Only when God reigns as King do his people find peace, purpose, and identity.

EXAMINATION

1. The pattern of rebellion and mercy

Judges began with disobedience. Israel failed to drive out the Canaanites, choosing coexistence over conquest. What seemed harmless tolerance became fatal influence. The idols of the land seduced their hearts, and the Lord's anger "burned against Israel." Yet whenever they cried out, he raised a deliverer.

Othniel established the pattern: the Spirit empowered him, victory came, and the land rested. Ehud, the left-handed assassin, delivered with cunning; Deborah inspired courage when men faltered; Gideon fought weakness with faith; Jephthah fought enemies but lost his daughter to foolish vows; Samson fought Philistines but lost himself to passion. Through each story, God's faithfulness outshined human failure. He remained the true Deliverer behind every judge.

Still, every victory was temporary. The land rested forty years, then forty more, but rest never lasted. Israel's repentance was shallow, and the cycle spun again. Sin's power proved stronger than human resolve. Judges reveals that what humanity needs is not a better hero but a new heart. Divine rescue demands more than momentary reform—it requires transformation.

2. The corruption of worship

By the time of Gideon and beyond, Israel's idolatry had moved from influence to institution. Gideon destroyed Baal's altar yet later crafted an ephod that became another snare. Micah's household shrine and the Levite's compromise in Judges 17-18 exposed the decay of faith itself. Religion remained, but revelation was forgotten. The people invoked God's name while violating his commands.

False worship always breeds moral confusion. When Micah said, "Now I know that the LORD will prosper me," he embodied the age's delusion—believing God's favor could rest on disobedience. The tribe of Dan institutionalized that same error, stealing Micah's idols and installing them as tribal gods. What began as private superstition became public apostasy. Judges shows that the greatest danger to faith is not atheism but imitation—worship that resembles truth while denying its authority.

3. The collapse of morality

The book's closing chapters, Judges 19-21, present moral disintegration in horrifying detail. The Levite's concubine, the civil war against Benjamin, and the abduction of women from Shiloh depict a society where conscience had died. The people who once cried against Canaanite cruelty now mirrored it. The absence of a king symbolized the absence of moral direction.

God's law had been replaced by personal preference. "Everyone did what was right in his own eyes." The phrase does not mean rebellion alone—it means relativism. Truth had become subjective. Religion was privatized, morality politicized, and justice weaponized. The covenant nation no longer looked distinct from its neighbors. Judges ended where Genesis 3 began—with people deciding for themselves what was good and evil.

4. The silence of God and the persistence of grace

Throughout the final chapters, God's voice was rare. He allowed his people to reap the fruit of self-rule. Yet his silence was not abandonment—it was discipline. Still, even amid judgment, mercy lingered. He preserved a remnant of Benjamin, sustained the line of promise, and kept his covenant alive. The story's very survival testifies to divine patience.

Every judge revealed both judgment and grace. God used flawed instruments to achieve his purposes, proving that deliverance depended not on human worth but divine faithfulness. His mercy outlasted their rebellion. Judges whispers the gospel long before the cross: salvation is never earned; it is given to undeserving sinners.

5. The longing for a king

By the book's end, Israel's cry for order foreshadowed the rise of monarchy. The people wanted stability, justice, and leadership. Yet their true need was not for a political ruler but for righteous sovereignty—God's rule embodied in a faithful king. The following books of Samuel and Kings would trace that longing through Saul's failure and David's imperfect reign, ultimately pointing to the Messiah.

The final verse of Judges stands as both indictment and invitation. Without a king, chaos reigned; with a human king, partial peace came; but only under the divine King will righteousness endure. Judges prepares the stage for the gospel by proving humanity's inability to save itself. Every flawed deliverer—Ehud, Deborah, Gideon, Samson—foreshadowed the perfect Deliverer who would come not merely to rescue from enemies but to redeem from sin.

APPLICATION

1. Without God's authority, chaos reigns

The refrain "everyone did what was right in his own eyes" remains the world's creed. Modern culture celebrates self-definition and moral autonomy, yet the outcome mirrors ancient Israel—confusion, division, and despair. When truth becomes relative, justice collapses. God's authority is not restriction but rescue. His Word sets boundaries that protect life and preserve peace. The lesson of Judges warns that freedom without submission is merely another form of bondage.

2. Sin's cycle can be broken only by transformation

Israel's repeated return to idolatry shows that deliverance without renewal fails. External victories cannot cure internal rebellion. The same Spirit who empowered the judges now indwells believers to break sin's cycle permanently (Gal. 5:15-22). Transformation begins when Christ reigns as Lord, replacing self-rule with Spirit-led obedience. God does not merely forgive our failures; He reshapes our hearts to love His ways.

3. Faith must be grounded in truth, not emotion

Micah's shrine and Gideon's ephod reveal religion driven by sentiment rather than Scripture. Sincerity is not a substitute for obedience. The church today must guard against worship that seeks experience without submission, comfort without conviction. Genuine faith conforms to God's revelation, not personal preference. To do what is "right in our own eyes" is to repeat Micah's sin with modern sophistication.

4. God's mercy endures despite human failure

Every page of Judges testifies to divine patience. God never ceased working, even through the flawed and faithless. He used reluctant Gideon, impulsive Jephthah, and compromised Samson to display his sovereignty. Christians can find hope that their failures need not define them. Grace rewrites stories. The God who refused to abandon Israel still restores his wandering people today.

5. The need for a true King

The moral chaos of Judges pointed toward the necessity of righteous kingship. Human deliverers offer temporary relief, but the heart demands divine reign. Christ fulfilled that longing as the perfect Judge and eternal King. He conquered not Midian or Philistia but sin and death. Where Judges end in ruin, the gospel begins in redemption. The invitation remains: surrender to the King who reigns not only over nations but within hearts.

CONCLUSION

Judges closes with silence and sorrow, but its message thunders through the ages: when people abandon God's rule, destruction follows. The book was not written merely to shock but to warn. It exposes the emptiness of human independence and the futility of moral relativism. Yet even amid ruin, grace whispers hope. The covenant God who endured Israel's rebellion would one day reign as King through his Son.

The phrase "no king in Israel" found its final answer in Jesus Christ. In him, the long search for righteous leadership ended. He is the Deliverer who breaks sin's cycle, the Judge who restores justice, and the King who rules by mercy. The book that began with conquest and ended in chaos finds completion at the cross—where rebellion met redemption.

For those who study Judges, the claion call is this: surrender every corner of life to the true King. Let no shrine of self-rule remain. Where he reigns, peace replaces confusion, holiness replaces compromise, and grace replaces guilt. The history of Judges may end in despair, but its theology ends in hope—hope fulfilled in Christ, through whom the words "everyone did what was right in his own eyes" are finally replaced with "every knee shall bow, and every tongue confess that Jesus Christ is Lord" (Phil. 2:11).

REFLECTION

1. How does Judges expose humanity's need for divine kingship?
2. What does the book teach about God's patience and justice?
3. Why did each judge's deliverance fail to bring lasting peace?
4. How does Christ fulfill what every judge lacked?
5. What lessons from Judges remain vital for believers today?

DISCUSSION

1. What modern examples reflect "everyone doing what is right in his own eyes"?
2. How can believers break sin's repeating patterns?
3. What distinguishes Spirit-led freedom from self-rule?
4. How does Christ's kingship answer the chaos of moral relativism?
5. What does it look like to live today under God's rule alone?

www.ingramcontent.com/pod-product-compliance
Lightning Source LLC
Chambersburg PA
CBHW052123070526
44586CB00016B/2051